# The Metaverse Dictionary

Words and meta-words for the Metaverse.

# THE
# METAVERSE DICTIONARY

Almost-Unabridged

## JOHN DALSTON

(Participant Observer)

THE METAVERSE DICTIONARY

Copyright © 2021 by John Dalston

All rights reserved. No part of this book may be reproduced in any form by any electronic or mechanical means (including photocopying, recording, or information storage and retrieval) without permission in writing from the publisher.

Published on Earth, in the United States of America
by AspectEdge, LLC., Florida.
www.AspectEdge.com

ISBN 978-0-9819579-2-0  (trade paperback)

Dedicated to thinking about what is beyond.

This page is obviously almost-blank.

# Introduction

Once almost-upon (nearly-beyond) a real time there was no Metaverse. Going back even further, there was no verse (or written history)—just imaginings of what things might be like in the future.

The prefix "meta-" came to the present day from an earlier time—between "verse" and "metaverse"–and is used in these ways and with these meanings:

**Meta-,** *prefix.* 1. Beyond, over, super, a higher level of generality, more comprehensive, more abstract, an umbrella term, overwhelming, governing, supervening, transcending, omnipresent. 2. After, later, more highly-organized, more specialized. 3. Virtual, inferred, expressing indirect evidence, being simulated. 4. Behind, changing, transforming, championing. 5. Under, supporting, more fundamental, and a priori (assumed, presupposed, preconceived). 6. Among (as in: in a relative position to an other), or with.

Not coincidentally, all of the above are also descriptions of perspectives that a mind and thinking can take.

In addition to this book being about the Metaverse, it is also partly about thinking about thinking.

History is replete with ideas and stories that feed into the current conception of what the Metaverse is and will become.

Some are already touting the Metaverse as the Internet version 3.0. From the perspective of the Internet then, the Metaverse has been growing gradually over a long time. But from the perspective of a bourgeoning new things called a Metaverse that is still trying to find it's legs, there are many things that might still change regarding even the fundamentals, like the following: what it will be called (if not the Metaverse), whether it will remain decentralized, what kinds of technologies might come into play, and what kinds of regulation might be needed.

It is for this reason that I expect that there will be future editions of this dictionary.

**Omniverse vs Metaverse**

The term Metaverse emphasizes that what is being discussed is something other than, and beyond the usual details, and jargon, and activity in physics, and chemistry, biological life, and industry; and also something beyond the social media sites, game sites, and shopping sites we have now.

Another contender for the name of the next iteration of the Internet is the Omniverse. Some look at things this way: that many Metaverses may exist within a Megaverse. Many Megaverses may exist within a Gigaverse. And many Gigaverses may exist within . . . ultimately, an Omniverse. Compared to "metaverse," the term "omniverse" more readily conveys the meaning that everything (omni) is involved (or will probably be involved in the future).

Either way, things are bound to be changing quickly.

**Terminology**

In this book, and for this edition, the use of the following will be common, and these seem to be good distinctions and categories to use: simulation, online game, shopping site, and meta-world.

Also used is the term "meta-platform;" and cloud-computing will be a big part of what is referred to here as "platform" and "meta-platform" and sometimes "support" or "network." The term "network" also refers to phone, cable, and satellite communications globally.

The lowercase "meta-world" is used to describe environments with metaverse-like attributes (and many exist now). The capitalized word "Metaverse" is used for both a) the whole world, and b) that part of the world that is Metaverse-related. Currently, the Metaverse is largely a decentralized phenomenon, but that will undoubtedly change.

Different terminologies and jargon will undoubtedly continue to emerge in different types of applications, with different programming languages or technologies being used, in different companies and business sectors, with different types of payments and currencies, in different nations, with different user age groups, or by location (Earth, Moon, Mars, or elsewhere).

The term virtual reality (VR) is used to describe an immersed experience (usually with some kind of headset) that might be used with a simulation or meta-world. The terms augmented reality (AR), or extended reality (XR) are associated with both special glasses and smart phones (and is associated with additional information that the internet can provide, including identifications, directions, and entertainment). Ordinary and personal computers and smart phones are also compatible with many simulations, online games, shopping sites, and meta-worlds.

## Simulations

Simulations are already used in many areas, including but not limited to physics, chemistry, biology and medicine, psychology, sociology, economics, politics, communicating, weather forecasting, pilot training, and in space-related and interplanetary scenarios.

## People

In dictionaries generally, the words "people" and "person" are defined to be broad terms, so meaning needs to further be taken from the context in which the word is used. They are not synonymous with the word "human." Here, the words "people" and "person" are used loosely, because things are changing rapidly.

We now have artificial beings that are smart. While one computer can beat a human at chess, others are busy replacing humans in the workplace. Smart things contain chips and AI software that make decisions, and help out in the real world. Our solar system is being explored first by non-humans. These "things" are on a gradual trend toward becoming people, even if they have not impressed us enough yet.

In the Metaverse, much of the actual thinking is being done by non-humans. The players are smart, *and* the environments are smart. With this in mind, the term "meta-person" is used here to refer to an actor that makes decisions in some part of the Metaverse (perhaps in a simulation, online game, shopping site, or meta-world). [See the definition of "Meta-person" below.]

There is a difference between "artificial intelligence" (smarts in one area of competence) and "general artificial intelligence" (what we might call real intelligence). The gray areas between these definitions are not addressed here. Also, partly because I expect these to change over time, I am leaving as out-of-scope any definition of the terms "artificial," "intelligence," and "smart."

For humans, the skull serves as a practical barrier to people sharing brain substance, and the architecture of the brain is such that it is always on (alternating only between sleep and awake modes). Smart things, however, will be able to augment themselves much more freely, adding and replacing capabilities and sensory apparatus as they determine to be necessary or desirable.

So the term "meta-person" *does* include the consideration of a person with respect to the Metaverse and includes smart things, and the term "person" does not include that additional consideration that the person necessarily be connected.

## Places

When talking about places we often need to consider context as well.

Here the term "the Metaverse" is juxtaposed with the term "the real world." Today, we are familiar with the term "the real world." We use it to to compare and contrast with some "fantasy world," or a possible future situations. But the Metaverse is already becoming the real world, and in the future that distinction will itself most-likely become an anachronism.

## Key Meta-terms

These meta-words, or meta-terms are used frequently, so it would help if you read these definitions first: Meta-layer, Meta-people, Meta-stuff, Meta-thing, Meta-world.

# Non-Meta words

**Agent,** *n.* One that acts or exerts power. Or, one that acts or exerts power for someone else.

**Avatar,** *n.* A representation, substitute, front, façade, mask, disguise, or continuation of and for a person. (As in, one manipulated by a computer user in an online game or an online shopping site.) Or, a meta-person being driven by a real person. [See Meta-avatar, Meta-person.]

**Blocky aesthetic,** *phrase,* A low-resolution, and possibly cheaply done aesthetic.

**Clone limit,** *phrase,* As soon as you start living, learning, and self-improving then you cease to be the same as your clone, so the clone limit in practical terms might better be called the "similar-limit" or the "almost-clone limit."

**Clone-limit,** *phrase,* There needs to be some way of limiting the number of non-biological beings on the planet. (This is an issue independent on any discussion about the Metaverse, but it does involve thinking outside-the-box, or meta-thinking.) Since before Thomas Malthus the limit for biological life was known to be capped by competition for consumable biological resources that have always been in limited supply. But non-biological life is not so constrained, and each berserker (large or small) may consume endlessly (or or not at all), depending on how it feels. Whether they are made in factories or clone themselves, one limiting factor to consider is the available mass/energy of planet Earth.

## The Metaverse Dictionary

**Deep fakes,** *phrase,* Alternate versions of real things, . . . or of fake things.

**Digital-twin,** *phrase,* Not you, but software that looks like you.

**Doppelganger,** *n.* A double. Not you, but someone who looks very much like you (perhaps indistinguishably so, and perhaps an alter ego).

**Filter Layer,** *n.* This is big, ancient, and ever-evolving. We have parents, censors, and government regulators. We have editors and publishers, and also air and water filters. These "filters" interface with each other and more and more will interface with the meta-filters that are part of the bourgeoning Metaverse.

**Funny money,** *n,* Money can be thought of as a "store of value" that exists somewhere (perhaps in the physical world, or in a bank's computer, or out there on in a Metaverse somewhere) and the type of money can be seen as having two coordinate values : 1) how reliable is it as a store of value, and 2) how strange it is. The more risky or unreliable it is, or the higher inflation is currently, the less the money might be considered a reliable store of value. The stranger the type of money it is, the less people are going to consider it seriously compared with other types of money. Therefore, the more unreliable and the more strange the money it is, one could say, the funnier it is, especially to those people who are not using it as a store of value.

**Gesture recognition,** *n.* The comprehension and understanding of what someone is doing with their body.

**Graphics chips,** *n.* Semiconductor chips that help a computer with it's thinking-type work.

**Malware,** *n.* Software used by cybercriminals to spy, and to steal information.

**Non-fungible tokens (NFTs),** *phrase,* Paraphernalia.

## The Metaverse Dictionary

**Process-freak,** *n.* A person that likes adding steps to a process that others must follow. Especially, someone that adds steps in front of where you are at in a process, . . . for everyone else's convenience.

**Professional visualization,** *phrase,* Seeing in the metaverse what must be.

**Ray-tracing,** *vt.,* A way of simulating light.

**Simulation,** *n.* One system functioning as if it were a different kind of system.

**Surveillance,** *n.* An information-gathering bonanza, and something everyone wants to do to everyone else.

**Teleportation,** *n.* Being there from afar.

**Tracking tags,** *n.* They enable people to keep track of things, and things to keep track of people.

**Trigger,** *n.* An event that initiates, or helps to cause other events. (Trigger point: The threshold at which that initiation happens. Trigger-happy: aggressively belligerent in attitude.) One thing leading to another thing. Many things lead to many other things. Etc.

**Ultra-Wideband (UWB),** *n.* Already in many chips, two-way conversations can happen between devices to triangulate positions with radio waves to get a centimeter-accurate sense of "where."

**Video-conference,** *n.* Online meeting.

*The Metaverse Dictionary*

This page is another almost-blank one.

*The Metaverse Dictionary*

# A

**Meta-able,** *adj.* Able to do something in a meta-world, or in the Metaverse generally, especially something that might not be possible in the real world.

**Meta-abrupt,** *adj.* A speed that is probably faster than a speeding bullet, but still slower than the speed of light.

**Meta-abs,** *n.* Avatar or Agent abdominal meta-muscles that are meta-firm or meta-chiseled/ribbed. Or, flabby abs in the real world that may look good because of some feature or app in the Metaverse. Most avatars would probably come with meta-abs straight out-of-the-box, figuratively speaking.

**Meta-absent,** *adj.* Not really absent, but appearing to be absent, simply because you can't see literally everyone who is watching and listening in.

**Meta-absolute,** *adj.* A variable that rarely changes much, or quickly.

**Meta-abstract,** *n., adj., v.* An abstraction of an abstraction. Then there's the meta-meta-abstract; that is really far out. Then there's the meta-meta-meta-abstract. Hmmm. [See Meta-understanding.]

**Meta-abundant,** *adj.* Maybe not so abundant in the real world, but plentiful and probably ubiquitous in a meta-world.

**Meta-abuse,** *n., v.t.* You'll take a lot of it, and love every minute of it. At least that's what they promise as you enter.

**Meta-abyss,** *n.* Just another one of Nietzsche's play-things. (Don't fall. You might miss.)

*The Metaverse Dictionary*

**Meta-academy,** *n.* Any school or meta-school where the unreal, fake stuff, or very profound stuff is taught. [See Meta-education, Meta-speak, Meta-method, Meta-way, Meta-art, Meta-stuff.]

**Meta-acceptable,** *adj.* Somewhere between "good enough for now" and "impossible to achieve because so many things depend on it," – and that is a wide spectrum and the acceptability depends on the situation. Simulations may have varying degrees of acceptability depending on the test.

**Meta-accident,** *n.* The kind of accident that can probably be cleaned up in less than a jiffy. (Probably no paperwork to fill out.)

**Meta-accounting,** *n., v.* Accounting that involves funny money. Or, accounting that involves very funny money. Or, accounting at such a high level that debits and credits no longer need to balance.

**Meta-achieve,** *v.* Achieve a position, goal, or status in a simulation, online game, shopping site, or in a meta-world.

**Meta-action,** *n.* Doing something in a meta-world that may or may not have consequences. The rule that "for every action there is an equal and opposite reaction" may not have been programmed in. If the reaction depends on settings and other conditions, the final outcome might be bizarre, unexpected, time-delayed, or never noticeable as far as anyone knows. Or, being. Or, becoming.

**Meta-active,** *adj.* Participating in some meta-environment. Or, not active, but records do not reflect inactivity yet. Or, affecting thought as a guiding principle, concept, or frame of reference.

**Meta-actor,** *n.* Someone who is paid to act in certain specific ways in a Simulation is called a "worker- bee." Someone who is paid to act in certain specific ways in certain meta-worlds, and that is required to join and become a member of the Meta-actors Meta-guild (MAMG) — the Metaverse equivalent of Hollywood Screen Actors Guild (SAG).

## The Metaverse Dictionary

**Meta-adjourn,** *v.* When a meeting dissolves and several people leave, . . . the meeting might actually still be going on, . . . you just never know.

**Meta-admiration,** *n.* Yes, you can always tell when they're serious — just like in real life.

**Meta-adobe,** *adj., n.* A home (or perhaps an office tower, supermarket, or bridge) made out of "adobe bricks" or "clay" and can behave just like "a real adobe structure," . . . but because it is made out of software it can also behave like anything else you might care to name.

**Meta-adolescent,** *n.* Anyone of any age who looks and acts like a gangly youth in a meta-world.

**Meta-adult,** *adj., n.* Someone who's meta-age is consistent with any of the algorithms and criteria that allow for things like being able to meta-vote, meta-kill during war-time, or have meta-sex. [See meta-age, meta-really-an-adult.]

**Meta-advice,** *n.* Advice that pertains to a particular meta-place. Or, advice about advice, like this recommendation, "You need to take the advice and then apply it to your particular situation, rather than just unquestioningly follow the advice verbatim."

**Meta-advisor,** *n.* Someone who specializes in giving advice that then needs to be interpreted in just the right way, . . . grasshopper.

**Meta-affluent,** *adj.* Someone who probably still needs to work for a living, but lives like royalty in a meta-world.

**Meta-affordable,** *adj.* Something that costs less funny money than you have and are willing to spend.

**Meta-age,** *n.* One's age in a simulation, or in a meta-world.

**Meta-Age,** *n.* That time on planet Earth during the current Cenozoic era and Quaternary period when the Holocene epoch splits into multiple real and imaginary parts. Or, when the Holocene epoch takes a bit of a turn, but no such divergence occurs.

**Meta-agenda,** *n.* An agenda that broader in scope (and possibly, that may not be entirely understood by all).

**Meta-agent,** *n.* The actor in meta-agency. A meta-agent may have advantageous or even super attributes or qualities, including: may interact with others instantly (so there is no waiting), may be able to understand and speak in all languages and accents, may never get tired (even though they may use that as an excuse), may continually improve and learn from their own mistakes and those of others, may be in many places at one time, and may be duplicated without limit. A meta-agent might act as the Brand Ambassador of a company, or as a meta-worker performing repetitive tasks. [See Meta-method, Meta-way.]

**Meta-agile,** *adj.* Very agile; but not as agile as to be meta-meta-agile.

**Meta-aim,** *v., n.* Adjust your settings, and hope for the best.

**Meta-air,** *n.* Bits and bytes, just like almost everything meta-else.

**Meta-alarming,** *adj.* Something that is surprising and unexpected for the reason that you didn't think that was even possible.

**Meta-alike,** *adj.* Meta-things that at least *seem* to be similar.

**Meta-alive,** *adj.* "Alive" by some accepted criteria, relatively speaking.

**Meta-almost,** *adv., adj.* Nearly getting there, or being the runner-up in a meta-world.

**Meta-alone,** *adj.* Not alone, but seeming to be alone.

**Meta-amazing,** *adj.* So impressive that you think it's unreal.

## The Metaverse Dictionary

**Meta-ambidextrous,** *adj.* Able to stretch out your right hand to competently have an effect anywhere in the world, and simultaneously to use you left hand with equal skill anywhere else in the world.

**Meta-ambiguous,** *adj.* A general or high-level concept or abstraction that is capable of being understood in two or more possible senses or ways.

**Meta-ambition,** *n.* The desire to create a splash in the Metaverse.

**Meta-amenities,** *n.* The equivalent of things like air-conditioning, running water, and parking that you might find in a meta-hotel in a meta-world. Or, the basics that you get in a cloud or meta-platform environment.

**Meta-American,** *n.* Anyone who lives over there, but works over here (in America) without commuting.

**Meta-ammo,** *n.* Bits and bytes that can, if need be, go as fast as a speeding bullet.

**Meta-amorphous,** *adj.* Something in a meta-world possessing the kind of shape, form, or structure that is very unorganized, or confusing.

**Meta-amount,** *n.* An amount of meta-stuff.

**Meta-anachronistic,** *adj.* Of a What happens when Meta-Aristotle meets Meta-Darwin, and Meta-Einstein, and they discuss George Jetson. Or, when Meta-Shakespeare rewrites the ending to Hamlet.

**Meta-analysis,** *n.* What you need to do before the meta-design stage, and the meta-development stage, and definitely before the meta-deployment stage. That's for meta-sure.

**Meta-ancient,** *adj.* Probably mostly real. [See Meta-old.]

**Meta-android,** *n.* An android, in a simulation or a meta-world. Or, a real fake human with all the right Metaverse access codes and passwords such that they can pretend to be a human working with real meta-androids in a simulation.

**Meta-angle,** *n.* Perhaps, and angle you hadn't counted on yet.

**Meta-animate,** *adj.* To move, in a most peculiar way.

**Meta-annul,** *v.t.* To cause to disappear, or pop-out of meta-existence. [See Meta-delete.]

**Meta-antithesis,** *n.* Real. Or, more concrete.

**Meta-applause,** *n.* Finally, now the sight and sound of one hand clapping is possible. The smell, touch, and taste of one hand clapping will be available in a future release.

**Meta-apply,** *v.* Just click on the "hand up" button.

**Meta-approve,** *v.* Just click on the "approve" button.

**Meta-approximate,** *adj.* Probably nearly near, or similar.

**Meta-arcade,** *n.* A place to play online games or join adventures into meta-worlds.

**Meta-archives,** *n.* Archives containing old audit logs and security related information, previous versions of meta-data and meta-stuff, and all those things that would just not fit in the current version.

**Meta-argument,** *n.* Two things disagreeing. Or, two people disagreeing in, or about a meta-world. Or two meta-people disagreeing anywhere.

**Meta-aristocracy,** *n.* Those who possess significant in control of meta-platforms, meta-worlds, lower meta-levels, or higher meta-vistas in the Metaverse. Or, anyone with lots of funny money. [See Meta-levels.]

**Meta-Aristotle,** *n.* An approximation of the person and personality of Aristotle created from all we know about him.

**Meta-arithmetic,** *n.* The adding, subtracting, multiplying, and dividing of things that perhaps one doesn't fully understand.

**Meta-armor,** *n.* Fake things that protect you from other fake things. Or, general concepts and ideas that protect you from other general concepts and ideas.

**Meta-army,** *n.* A formidable meta-force, comprised of mostly . . . of who-knows-what. Or, a practically weightless show of momentous force.

**Meta-arrest,** *v.t., n.* When a policeman reads you your rights, and then something happens, and the policeman takes off like a flash after someone else.

**Meta-arrgh,** *interj.* I think I agree with your general premise. Or, I am getting impatient with meta-stuff. Or, I am reservedly optimistic about the idea of our not having to meet in person. (As uttered by a Meta-pirate.)

**Meta-arson,** *n.* The act of creating red, orange, and yellow meta-stuff that then moves in such a way that causes many meta-things of many different wavelengths to suddenly behave differently than they used to before the red, orange, and yellow meta-stuff arrived.

**Meta-art,** *n., adj.* Perhaps, Non-fungible tokens (NFTs).

**Meta-artificial,** *adj.* Perhaps, a tautology.

**Meta-artist,** *n.* A maker/producer/creator of Meta-art.

**Meta-ask,** *v.* Just click on the "hand up" button. [Same as in Meta-apply.]

## The Metaverse Dictionary

**Meta-asleep,** *adj.* How you will probably find you avatar after an exhausting day.

**Meta-aspect,** *n.* A phenomenon or facet peculiar to a simulation, meta-world, or Metaverse.

**Meta-assembly,** *n.* A collection of meta-stuff.

**Meta-athletic,** *adj.* Almost-infinitely fit, strong, and supple. [See Meta-fit.]

**Meta-atmosphere,** *n.* An atmosphere that probably consists of mostly transparent bits and bytes. One that doesn't need to be breathable, per se. Or, the atmosphere surrounding deep thinkers, especially a room full of deep thinkers.

**Meta-atomism,** *n.* A whole new theory of the meta-small.

**Meta-attended,** *v.* Heard or saw something for at least a split second, maybe longer.

**Meta-attention,** *n.* The kind of attention that can be spread out all over the Metaverse.

**Meta-attractive,** *adj.* Attractive in a way that something real cannot possibly be.

**Meta-attribution,** *n.* At first, perhaps, to attribute deep things like goals, abilities, and other characteristics only based on the superficial things that are more immediately obvious.

**Meta-auction,** *v.t., n.* An auction of Meta-stuff (perhaps, Meta-art, or Meta-shirts).

**Meta-audience,** *n.* What you do is sure to be observed by more people than you think, and in different contexts, and at later times than you might expect.

*The Metaverse Dictionary*

**Meta-audit,** *v.t., n.* There will be those that contribute to reliable audit ability, and those that try to obfuscate and deceive . . . just like in the real world.

**Meta-audition,** *n.* A simulation, and where you can practice you audition. ("They" may still be watching.)

**Meta-authoritative,** *adj.* Speaking forcefully, probably knowledgeably, and probably from a distance.

**Meta-authority,** *n.* An authority with understanding and/or control of meta-stuff in the Metaverse.

**Meta-autonomy,** *n.* Autonomy is an illusion, and that goes doubly so in a Metaverse — where stakeholders, and the meta-aristocracy, and those in the meta-levels can be more easily manipulate everyone's life. [See Meta-aristocracy, Meta-level.]

**Meta-available,** *adj.* Available to those that meet certain criteria (based on privileges, settings, demographics, or meta-demographics).

**Meta-avatar,** *n.* An avatar that an avatar uses. An avatar that uses an avatar.

**Meta-award,** *n.* A fake award for something unreal.

# B

**Meta-babe,** *n.* We can't all look babe-like. But maybe we can in the Metaverse. But there still might be pressures to differentiate oneself from the crowd. Then again, one's avatar might become part of one's official identity, and so it might look more like a Driver's License, and be regulated to the hilt.

**Meta-babies,** *n.* These will probably pop up out of nowhere all the time, and then go away, or . . . who knows what will happen to most meta-babies. They will probably not be delivered by a stork. The avatars of real human babies will probably be persistent, and will need to be updated as the real child grows. So meta-babies might grow and learn over time. For security reasons, it may be that most people appear to be meta-babies.

**Meta-bachelor,** *n.* Someone who appears to be male and unmarried, at least in some circumstances.

**Meta-backward,** *adv., adj.* Meta-forward if you are facing the other way. Or, without having the most-current meta-gear or meta-knowledge.

**Meta-bad,** *adj.* Destructive or anti-social, but only in a meta-environment.

**Meta-balanced,** *adj.* Seeming to be fine.

**Meta-balloon,** *n.* Probably the most useful thing in any meta-world, at least when you first arrive, is to see meta-balloons floating around. That might indicate a lot about the type of space you are in — such as meta-predictability and meta-safety. A trial-balloon might float by in front of you, and you could pop it and see what happens. Maybe you bring in your own trial balloon. If it pops in the wrong way, you might need to play with the settings (yours, the baloon's, your avatar's, or the ones you set in such a hurry on the way in).

**Meta-ballot,** *n.* The kind of meta-thing that may come in handy during an election, or meta-election.

**Meta-balmy,** *adj.* The type of meta-weather that may or may not suggest to your avatar that it's time to change into that Hawaiian meta-shirt.

**Meta-bamboozled,** *adj.* Potentially, the state everyone will be in eventually.

**Meta-banana,** *n.* Unlike a real banana, it contains no potassium; but it still might contain meta-potassium (m-K).

**Meta-band,** *n.* A band of agent-musicians that are not real, and so they can just keep playing and playing. They work cheap, and they know almost-all of the songs.

**Meta-bank,** *n.* A good meta-place for funny money.

**Meta-bankrupt,** *adj.* Out of funny money.

**Meta-bar,** *n.* A bar where something is fake. Perhaps the beer, wine, and liquor only look real from a distance. Or, maybe the bartender is fake, but the drinks are real. Or, maybe the bartender and the drinks are real, and the customers are fake (a training simulation for bartenders). Or, maybe the bartender and the drinks are fake, but the customers are real (an el cheapo wedding or work Xmas party). Or, maybe the bartender, the drinks, and the customers are fake, but the police are real (a law enforcement simulation.) [You still might get carded.]

**Meta-basic,** *n.* Probably, something stable and reliable. Maybe, something simple and ubiquitous. Probably, something many rely on. Maybe a part of a meta-world or meta-platform.

**Meta-beach,** *n.* A quasi-sandy spot.

**Meta-beautiful,** *adj.* The easier it will be to fake appearances, the more people will try to distinguish themselves from the crowd by appearing in different ways, and the more people will need to try to look under the hood. Just below the surface that other meta-person might be a clunky algorithms, or mostly a "third party" (perhaps an insurance company, or an OEM hardware manufacturer, . . . for your convenience).

**Meta-because,** *conj.* For a reason, but one that may, or may not make sense.

**Meta-bed,** *n.* A meta-thing that is typically bigger than a meta-sleeping bag, and smaller than a meta-bedroom, that your avatar or some agent may or may not want to meta-lie meta-down meta-on.

**Meta-bedraggled,** *adj.* It's all for show.

**Meta-beef,** *n.* Fake meat, of a type that is comparatively more meta-chewy than meta-potatoes.

**Meta-behavior,** *n.* Typically, more complicated than real behavior, and often less predicable.

**Meta-being,** *v.i.* Acting.

**Meta-benefit,** *v.t., n.* The use of simulations provide a way to get through a process without having to do it for real (when prototyping or experimenting). Simulations can run faster, and probably do not need to be run in full every time. For businesses of all types this can save both time and money. The down-side of the cost of initial setup can partially be offset with the use of the "copy" feature.

**Meta-bias,** *n.* A leaning in the Meta-way.

**Meta-bicycle,** *n.* Any bicycle built for more than two or three (and maybe, as many as the largest finite number you can think of).

## The Metaverse Dictionary

**Meta-bilked,** *adj.* When your funny money disappears, and you know someone tricked you to get it, but you have absolutely no idea how they did it.

**Meta-billing,** *n.* Not on the marquee, but still used in promotions.

**Meta-biology,** *n.* A complex subject, and the foundation of meta-medicine — based on meta-biochemistry, meta-chemistry, and meta-physics.

**Meta-birth,** *n.* When something pops into existence. Or, when something pops into existence, but for one of you it wasn't quite so much of a surprise.

**Meta-blacklist,** *n.* The Information Age enhanced the power of the "the list," used as never before, and as a power weapon. Are you in? Or, are you definitely out? And power weapons die hard. But expect lists of people to be used less and less as algorithms and AI takes over in smarter and smarter ways, and as smart things make up their own lists in real-time using their own perspective, and using the very latest available information.

**Meta-blackmail,** *n., v.t.* Advertizing. Or, messages of any kind. For every action or non-action there may be a similar, or dissimilar, or delayed response that you may or may not notice, . . . considering the convenience of all the stakeholders that might be somewhat involved.

**Meta-blameless,** *adj., n.* "The meta-layers made me do it." [See Meta-layer.] [See Meta-responsible.]

**Meta-blanket,** *n.* If you can't find one, just use a large meta-towel.

**Meta-blarney,** *n.* Exaggerated flattery about general ideas and concepts. Or, exaggerated flattery about a simulation, online game, shopping experience, or meta-world.

## The Metaverse Dictionary

**Meta-blend,** *n.* A blend of things that might be more disparate or more abstract than you might expect.

**Meta-blind,** *adj.* Poorly-sighted or sightless in one or more fake place. Check your settings. Maybe it's you're security privileges. Maybe the meta-world has not paid it's bills lately. Maybe the simulation is still under construction. You may need to ask for meta-help.

**Meta-block,** *v.t., n.* Hinder, covertly.

**Meta-bottleneck,** *n.* A slowdown because of a constraint that isn't really a constraint (like when there is a disturbance off to the side of the road).

**Meta-bottom,** *n.* A place from which you can clearly see the bottom.

**Meta-bound,** *adj.* Something stuck in a meta-world.

**Meta-bounded,** *n.* A place completely surrounded by meta-places. [See Meta-limit.]

**Meta-boyfriend,** *n.* A guy that you have only just started to meta-date, but have not actually met yet.

**Meta-break,** *n.* Taking a break from the real world by doing something in the Metaverse.

**Meta-brink,** *n.* Where a meta-place ends.

**Meta-builder,** *n.* A builder of Meta-things. [See Meta-method.]

**Meta-built,** *adj.* Designed but not built. Or, pie in the sky. [See Meta-method, Meta-way.]

**Meta-bullshit,** *n.* Kinda similar to the real "crap of bull," but more abstract or complicated. Perhaps, a little poopy in intent.

## The Metaverse Dictionary

**Meta-burglar,** *n.* Someone who steals information or changes something without ever entering the building. [See also, Meta-burgle.]

**Meta-burgle,** *v.t.* Breaking into a meta-place in order to remove meta-stuff.

**Meta-businessman,** *n.* A business person who makes money on meta-stuff, in a meta-world, or in some way because the Metaverse exists.

**Meta-butt,** *n.* Any butt with more than one crack is probably a meta-butt.

**Meta-buy,** *v.t.* The exchange of funny money for funny stuff.

**Meta-buzz,** *n.* The buzz heard 'round the world. Or, that little chirping sound you can't get rid of.

# C

**Meta-cage,** *n.* A cage from which one can easily escape just by turning off one's computer. Or, perhaps, a planet from which one can never escape.

**Meta-calendar,** *n.* A calendar in a simulation. Or, the Metaverse calendar.

**Meta-captioned,** *adj.* The words that are sometimes included underneath or associated with things, commercial products, places, or meta-people as you encounter them, either in an AR or VR situation.

**Meta-capture,** *v.t.* In a simulation, the way to move something into a different setting.

**Meta-car,** *n.* A "connected" car. Or, a smart car. Perhaps, not just transportation, but a car that can also help with many of the other aspects of your life, . . . for your convenience.

**Meta-carbon,** *n.* One of the many fake elements (m-C).

**Meta-career,** *n.* A career where most of the work is performed in a meta-world. [See Meta-field.]

**Meta-caricature,** *n.* Perhaps, one of the available settings on your avatar. Or, a meta-agent that might seem more complex once you got to know him, or her, or it.

**Meta-cart,** *n.* Where you put your meta-stuff while you are still shopping.

## The Metaverse Dictionary

**Meta-case,** *n.* The case you are working on in your simulation as a trial lawyer. Or, that thing with a handle on it that your meta-world came in. It could become useful again if you want to move your meta-world somewhere else.

**Meta-cause,** *n.* Perhaps, the cause of the cause. When something happens in a meta-world then you may or may not know how or why that thing happened, depending on how that meta-world was designed and built.

**Meta-cave,** *n.* Perhaps, not a feature but a hole in the software. Beware.

**Meta-censorship,** *n.* Xxxxxxx.

**Meta-century,** *n.* The one starting in the year 2000, very early in the morning, when real people were dreaming about what the future might be like.

**Meta-certainties,** *n.* Deletions, and tax-deferral schemes.

**Meta-chair,** *n.* Anything someone can sit on in a meta-world.

**Meta-chicken,** *n.* It's better for you than real free-range grilled chicken, and better for you than plant-based chicken, . . . but only if you can stomach the stuff.

**Meta-children,** *n.* Rug-rats, being monitored by their parents perhaps.

**Meta-circumstances,** *n.* Circumstances that you can easily avoid. Or, circumstances that you just can't escape.

**Meta-circus,** *n.* A sideshow that everyone can see.

**Meta-city,** *n.* A meta-place that is larger and more populated than a meta-village or meta town, but smaller than a whole meta-world. It may have a meta-nightlife. It may have an average noon-time temperature. It probably has it's own evening news broadcast, . . . and suburbs.

**Meta-civil,** *adj.* How most people are to most other people most of the time.

**Meta-civilized,** *adj.* Most meta-worlds will probably evolve their own social norms, and customs, and meta-rules. Probably, many meta-worlds will borrow norms, and customs, and rules from the real world. How civilized things are anywhere will probably change over time; just look at what happened to the real world. Meta-tea and meta-biscuits anyone.

**Meta-clean,** *adj.* Simulations meant for the training of janitors, garbage men, and those cleaning up space junk might not be clean, but, especially out-of-the box, probably most other simulations would be light on the fake dirt and thrown away wrappers.

**Meta-cloak,** *n.* Something in a meta-world that conceals.

**Meta-clock,** *n.* The timepiece on the blue wall at the very end of a meta-world. Or, anything that can measure fake-time.

**Meta-close,** *adj., v.t.* Near or almost in some meta-way.

**Meta-clothing,** *n.* What an avatar or meta-agent wears during the day, especially when out and about. Or, any real clothing with the word "meta" on it. [See Meta-shirt.]

**Meta-clumsy,** *adj.* Clumsy like a fox.

**Meta-coercion,** *n.* To cause something to happen that causes something else to happen from a safe distance. [See Meta-level.]

**Meta-coffee,** *n.* That which gets one going in the morning in a meta-world. Every environment needs it's own type of stimulant.

## The Metaverse Dictionary

**Meta-company,** *n.* Almost any company that doesn't exist in the real world. Or, a Metaverse company.

**Meta-conceal,** *v.t.* To hide in a meta-level. [See Meta-level.]

**Meta-concept,** *n.* A vague or too high-level objective perception.

**Meta-confess,** *v.t.* To confess to a lesser charge. Or, to just *look* guilty without saying anything.

**Meta-console,** *v.t.* What you get to help you run a simulation or meta-world.

**Meta-constant,** *adj.* A variable.

**Meta-consumable,** *n.* Something that is only partially consumed (banana, mango, coconut).

**Meta-consumer,** *n.* Someone waiting for the price to go down. Or, someone waiting for their next paycheck. Or, a producer doing a field study.

**Meta-convergence,** *n.* When meta-worlds collide.

**Meta-conversation,** *n.* A few words with someone that potentially anyone or everyone can hear.

**Meta-cop,** *n.* Law enforcement in a meta-world.

**Meta-copy,** *n., v.* Probably, and easy copy to make. [See Meta-contagious, Meta-mutate.]

**Meta-correct,** *adj.* Correct for or within the environment.

**Meta-counterfeit,** *adj., n.* A fake fake.

**Meta-country,** *n.* A meta-nation in a meta-world.

## The Metaverse Dictionary

**Meta-couple,** *n.* An informally-linked pair. Or, a formally linked pair, generally speaking. Or, two meta-worlds.

**Meta-covered,** *adj.* Having information about you visible in some way to other people nearby. Perhaps visible meta-tags, or text-messages of things that might be useful to know, like "dog-lover," or "pedophile," or "vaccinated," or "millionaire." These will probably be available by settings and privileges, and the settings and privileges of others.

**Meta-craft,** *n.* A skill that is useless in the real world, but that is useful in a simulation or meta-world.

**Meta-crash,** *v.t.* What happens when fake things go bump in the night.

**Meta-creative,** *adj.* Those Meta-dedicated to making sure the world doesn't repeat itself. Or, those creating Meta-stuff and speaking Meta-speak in Meta-new Meta-ways. [See Meta-mutate, Meta-stuff, Meta-speak.]

**Meta-credentials,** *n.* A document or meta-document showing that one is capable of making serious change happen in a meta-world. [See Meta-certificate.]

**Meta-creep,** *v.i., n.* A strange and undesirable meta-person.

**Meta-critical,** *adj.* An essential ingredient in order for meta things to exist, like: a meta-world, a meta-platform, or a Metaverse.

**Meta-criticism,** *n.* Criticism about what is behind or supporting a thing or meta-thing. Or, criticism about a simulation, online game, shopping site, or a meta-world.

**Meta-curious,** *adj.* Curious about the Metaverse, or something related to it in some way. Or, curious as to what is behind or supporting a thing or meta-thing. [See Meta-level.]

*The Metaverse Dictionary*

**Meta-current,** *adj.* Whenever "now" is in a simulation – which might be a very different time from "now" in real life.

**Meta-customer,** *n.* Any customer you haven't met in person yet. Or, Earth.

# D

**Meta-dabble,** *v.* To be mildly or occasionally interested in a meta-world in some ways. Perhaps, one's interactions with the Metaverse appear to be desultory.

**Meta-danger,** *n.* Danger, in a simulation or meta-world, or otherwise involving the Metaverse.

**Meta-dark,** *adj.* What you get when someone turns the lights out in a meta-world, or the Metaverse.

**Meta-Darwin,** *n.* A hypothetical (now) meta-personality of Charles Darwin created from all we know about him.

**Meta-data,** *n.* Bits and bytes from somewhere strange. Or, data that is about something high-level.

**Meta-date,** *v.t., n.* The date in your simulation or meta-world (which may not be today, or even in our current Holocene epoch).

**Meta-day,** *n.* The length of time equivalent to one day in a simulation, no matter how long it takes wall-clock time.

**Meta-dead,** *adj.* Probably still alive, and still kicking. Even really dead and from a long time ago people can be meta-young in the Metaverse. Or, one who as just died in this run of a simulation, and who will be alive again the moment you re-start the simulation.

**Meta-deadline,** *n.* A deadline that someone else just pulled out of their hat. Where did that one come from?

**Meta-death,** *n.* What happens when a meta-person stops using up computing resources.

**Meta-December,** *n.* December, just like in the real world. Just, in your simulation it can happen at any time.

**Meta-decidable,** *adj.* Decidable within a meta-world, without involving externalities.

**Meta-declassify,** *v.t.* To set free form the current structures of classification. Perhaps, to delist, or hide.

**Meta-deconstruct,** *v.t.* To tease apart what happened in the Metaverse. To tease apart events that might happen in the future in the Metaverse. [See Meta-meant, Meta-understanding.]

**Meta-deed,** *n.* A particular action taken, or something done in a meta-world. Or, an action taken, or something done in a meta-level. [See Meta-level.]

**Meta-deep,** *adj.* So deep that there are serious loose ends in thought still. Or, *not* deep enough.

**Meta-defective,** *adj.* Anything defective in such a way that you can't fix it.

**Meta-delegate,** *v.t.* To assign work to an avatar or meta-agent.

**Meta-delete,** *v.t.* To cause meta-stuff to not exist, while still leaving a audit trail (of course), . . . for everyone's convenience.

**Meta-dig,** *v.* To dig into thinking more deeply, or in new place. Or, to ask questions about things that might be perceived as none of your business.

**Meta-display,** *v.t.* A huge industry.

**Meta-divorce,** *n.* A divorced that happens over the internet, . . . for everyone's convenience.

*The Metaverse Dictionary*

**Meta-doctor,** *n.* A doctor that you've never seen in person. [See Meta-education.]

**Meta-documented,** *adj.* Words over there that somewhat resemble what you really see over here.

**Meta-dogma,** *n.* The protective layer of related facts, traditions, and discriminating principles that you typically find around dogma.

**Meta-domestic,** *adj.* A nice fake house, with a nice fake family, and a nice fake dog or cat. Optional, a nice fake backyard too.

**Meta-dreaming,** *v.i.* Dreaming or daydreaming about somewhere in a simulation or meta-world.

**Meta-drunk,** *adj.* Seemingly, to have little immediate control over where one is going in the Metaverse. Perhaps, because one is physically drunk.

**Meta-dull,** *adj.* Not very well-defined.

**Meta-dumping,** *n.* Uploading data en masse.

**Meta-duty,** *n.* Like "heavy duty," but in a meta-world. To be further defined in the circumstances.

**Meta-dystopia,** *n.* Any simulation, or meta-world, or place in the Metaverse that meta-people might be inclined to avoid.

# E

**Meta-eavesdrop,** *v., v.i.* To hide out in a meta-layer and just observe. Or, to observe from somewhere else where one can't be seen, or to observe but later and not in real-time in such a way that the participants are unaware. [See Meta-layer.]

**Meta-economize,** *v.t.* To save money by using a simulation. Or, to save money by spying on others.

**Meta-economy,** *n.* That part of the economy that is more *about* the economy or *beyond* the economy from a practical perspective. Or, that part of the economy that consists of fake stuff and funny money. Or, an economy consisting mostly of fake stuff and funny money.

**Meta-editor,** *n.* Whoever changes your work without you knowing about it.

**Meta-educational,** *adj.* Educational in the same way that television and the internet is educational.

**Meta-effect,** *n., v.t.* An effect caused by a simulation, a meta-world, or the Metaverse, especially a previously-unexpected effect.

**Meta-effective,** *adj.* Probably, more effective. At least, probably more visible, or having further reach.

**Meta-egregious,** *adj.* Something in or about the Metaverse that is so outrageously bad that it might make the evening Meta-news.

**Meta-Einstein,** *n.* A hypothetical (now) meta-personality of Albert Einstein created from all we know about him.

## The Metaverse Dictionary

**Meta-element,** *n.* Any one of the made-up elements (ones not on the Periodic Table). For Perhaps, elements that are necessary for a particular meta-world to exist. Perhaps, Almostium. [See Meta-atomism.]

**Meta-employ,** *v.t.* To hire someone who is not a human, especially someone who is not real and does not have much of a physical presence. It will interesting to see meta-employees juggle the demands from multiple stakeholders.

**Meta-engaged,** *adj.* People A riddle wrapped in an enigma, in meta-world.

**Meta-enter,** *v.t.* Poke your meta-nose in and take a quick look around.

**Meta-entitlement,** *n.* When you're entitled to something until someone else decides differently.

**Meta-entertainment,** *n.* The kind of entertainment that might keep you avatar, an AI-agent, or other meta-person glued to the Metaverse. Or, Meta-stuff that is found to be amusing to mostly-real people.

**Meta-enchilada,** *n.* A practically-weightless, and therefore almost-healthy, tiny morsel of "food" that you can't eat, because it's made out of software.

**Meta-estate,** *n.* The total of what one "owns" in the Metaverse.

**Meta-erase,** *v.t.* The same as meta-delete, unless its snot. But to leave around the audit logs, and the backups, and everything else that is required to be kept. [See Meta-delete.]

**Meta-evidence,** *n.* Evidence that hasn't been deleted yet. Or, from the meta-archives, evidence that is probably pertinent and reliable.

*The Metaverse Dictionary*

**Meta-ethics,** *n.* Values are up there somewhere. Relative ethics. The kind of ethics that almost-naturally falls between "anything goes," and "everything is mine to do with as I please."

**Meta-excess,** *n.* Too much of a meta-thing.

**Meta-exchange,** *v.t.* When you exchange any meta-thing for any other meta-thing. Or, when you exchange a meta-thing for funny money, or vice versa.

**Meta-exhibit,** *n.* An exhibit of Meta-art, Meta-speak, or other Meta-stuff. [See Meta-art, Meta-speak, Meta-stuff, Meta-world.]

**Meta-exhibitionist,** *n.* Anyone and everyone, in the Metaverse. Or, someone who likes to show off their Meta-stuff.

**Meta-expendable,** *adj.* Anyone you can delete without getting in trouble for doings so.

**Meta-expert,** *adj., n.* Someone making the big bucks.

**Meta-expired,** *adj.* In the archive.

**Meta-extortion,** *v.t.* Perhaps something to be avoided, in situations where you get 0-privacy and 0-trust, and some people are much more private and trusted.

**Meta-extrovert,** *n.* Even if someone is normally quiet, they still might raise a ruckus in a simulation or meta-world.

# F

**Meta-face,** *n., v.* Your meta-face might be photo-realistic, or it might be your avatar's face. It might be a caricature, look blocky, or look like someone else. The meta-people you meet will have the same range of possibilities available to them.

**Meta-facility,** *n.* A place that houses the equipment to support a simulation, online game, shopping site, or a meta-world.

**Meta-fact,** *n.* A fact about something beyond what is there. Or, a fact about a simulation, or a meta-world, and one that might change.

**Meta-factor,** *n.* A pesky little variable in a formula or algorithm that makes a difference for a meta environment, or for the real world as it relates to something in the Metaverse. Or, the large and beneficial change something in the Metaverse brings.

**Meta-faculty,** *n.* The innate or acquired ability to act in a simulation, online game, shopping site, or or meta-world. Or, the teaching and senior administrators in an educational institution that does not teach in-person.

**Meta-fail,** *v.i.* A practice run, in a simulation.

**Meta-failure,** *n.* Someone who is a failure at being a failure.

**Meta-fair,** *adj.* Fair, as far as you know (because the behind-the-scenes actions may compensate for what otherwise might seem unfair, or the other way around.)

**Meta-fake,** *adj.* A fake fake. Or, a very general or high-level kind of fake.

## The Metaverse Dictionary

**Meta-famous,** *adj.* Famous within a meta-world. Or, more famous than most in the Metaverse.

**Meta-fan,** *n.* Someone who "follows" you around in the Metaverse. Or, what might be installed in the ceiling of your meta-house.

**Meta-far,** *adj.* Appearing to be at a great distance.

**Meta-farm,** *n.* Where meta-things are grown, rather than invented.

**Meta-fashionable,** *adj.* Strange, just for the sake of being different.

**Meta-fear,** *n.* Fear of the known unknown, and of the unknown unknown. Or, fear of all of the things that are known, but not known to you, and that do pertain to you, and that are influencing you, but the details are being kept from you, . . . for their convenience, . . . for your convenience.

**Meta-feast,** *n.* A large meal, mostly made out of bits and bytes.

**Meta-feel,** *v.i.* Feel through your avatar.

**Meta-female,** *adj.* Anyone (male, female, or a any kind of meta-person).

**Meta-fickle,** *adj.* Steadfast in your open-mindedness.

**Meta-fiction,** *n.* When the names have been changed, but the story really did happen.

**Meta-field,** *n.* Any yard, in the Metaverse. Or, that multifarious arena that produces such things as simulations, online games, shopping sites, meta-worlds, meta-platforms.

**Meta-fight,** *v.t.* Fight is such a way that nobody gets physically hurt. Perhaps, to assail each other with words. Or, to metaphorically stand one's ground. [See Meta-war.]

*The Metaverse Dictionary*

**Meta-figure,** *n., v.i.* Like a stick figure, an avatar or meta-agent might appear to be quite simple before they get "fleshed-out" with a meta-body, meta-clothing, meta-equipment, and the latest security updates.

**Meta-filling,** *n., v.t.* A dentist filling a tooth over the internet. Or, a simulation of doing a filling. Perhaps your dentist would like to practice a complicated procedure before really practicing his profession on you.

**Meta-filter,** *v.t.* What you need to keep you sane. Filtering it all out might become illegal, but do your best.

**Meta-final,** *adj.* The end of one story or world, and the beginning of something new. The closer we get to an end, the more like a new beginning it becomes.

**Meta-find,** *v.t.* When you know that it is going to be in the last place you look, and it ends up being inside a computer.

**Meta-fine,** *adj.* High resolution.

**Meta-flaw,** *n.* Probably nothing to worry about, in that it will be addressed in order of priority, like a pothole of a certain diameter and depth.

**Meta-Florida,** *n.* That part of Florida that is above the dirt. Also, that part of Florida that gets the most respect.

**Meta-foggy,** *adj.* Both too high-level and confusing.

**Meta-folk,** *n.* Meta-people, especially of the common variety (even when the commonality is limited to a locality, or a meta-world).

**Meta-follow,** *v.* Follow from a distance, and maybe without anyone knowing (including who is being followed).

**Meta-food,** *n.* I taste like data, but acts on you like catnip.

## The Metaverse Dictionary

**Meta-force,** *v.t., n.* Perhaps, the next force in the American military, after Cyber Force, and Space Force.

**Meta-forget,** *v.t.* What happens when memory gets wiped out.

**Meta-form,** *n., v.* Any one of Plato's forms, plus any new ones you might find in the Metaverse.

**Meta-frame,** *n., v.* That which surrounds an imagined Meta-scene. Or, the frame of understanding for what you see, where someone else might have a different perspective.

**Meta-freak,** *n.* Who isn't. Now.

**Meta-friends,** *n.* Friends who you would not have run into except for the Metaverse.

**Meta-fun,** *n.* The fun you have discussing what happened to you in a simulation, playing an online game, visiting a shopping site, or entering a meta-world.

**Meta-fundamental,** *adj.* The three R's. Or any 101 class. Or, physics and technology.

**Meta-future,** *adj., n.* Whatever is going to happen in the simulation. It may or may not seem like you are in a Time Machine.

**Meta-fuzzy,** *adj.* Exceedingly difficult to understand.

*The Metaverse Dictionary*

# G

**Meta-gadget,** *n.* A doohickey that does whatever, as defined by the software that makes it.

**Meta-gaffe,** *n.* Not nearly as embarrassing as a real gaffe. Or, much more embarrassing than a real gaffe.

**Meta-gambit,** *n.* A gambit that involves a meta-situation. Or, a gambit that involves pitting real against fake in some way, in the hopes that one side will win. [See Meta-method, Meta-way.]

**Meta-game,** *n.* Any game meta-people play. Or, any online game real people play.

**Meta-gap,** *n.* The gap between "the real world" and the Metaverse. Or, the gap between two different meta-worlds.

**Meta-garbage,** *n.* Most of the stuff in any meta-world is meta-garbage – but because one meta-man's meta-garbage is another man's meta-gold, you probably won't be able to just delete it.

**Meta-garden,** *n.* A meta-garden might be so large a place that meta-worlds can be grown there, or as small as an almost-insignificant portion of meta-land behind a meta-house. Or, the "meta-civilized" version of a meta-jungle. Or, any fake place where the butterfly effect is more noticeable than gravity. A meta-garden may or may not have meta-grass, or meta-lawn furniture.

**Meta-meta-gear,** *n.* T-shirts, tents, pens, or other objects in a meta-world that have meta-slogans on them. [See Meta-slogan.]

**Meta-geek,** *n.* A person who spends considerable time with the details of one or more meta-worlds, or the whole Metaverse.

## The Metaverse Dictionary

**Meta-genius,** *n.* Clever in ways you'll never understand.

**Meta-genuine,** *adj.* A real or good fake. Perhaps, a non-fungible tokens (NFT).

**Meta-generous,** *adj.* Someone who gives away gobs of pretend stuff.

**Meta-giraffe,** *n.* Maybe a meta-zebra pretending to be a meta-giraffe.

**Meta-girlfriend,** *n.* A girl that you have only just started to meta-date, but have not actually met yet.

**Meta-glamour,** *n.* The exciting and often illusory and romantic attractiveness of general ideas and concepts.

**Meta-global,** *adj.* Anything that pertains to most of the globe, most countries, most of the important countries (according to your estimation), or most of the people.

**Meta-golf,** *n.* A golf game played over eighteen holes in a single meta-world.

**Meta-gravity,** *n.* Whatever is pulling the Metaverse together. You can almost feel it.

**Meta-gregarious,** *adj.* A meta-person or agent (especially a sales agent) that appears sociable, affable, amiable, friendly, or talkative.

**Meta-group,** *n.* A bunch or gaggle of meta-people.

**Meta-growth,** *n.* Simulated growth. Or, growth by acquisition.

**Meta-guzzle,** *v.t.* To act like one is drinking a lot, in an environment where one is actually not drinking at all.

# H

**Meta-habit,** *n.* A habit that can be changed in an instant, with new software.

**Meta-hack,** *v.t.* It will be up to each meta-platform to prevent certain types of problems, and then the meta-place "owners" to prevent certain other types of problems, but it will be up to everyone individually to buy enough protection such that their own meta-life will be tolerable. Same as now, the hackers and cyber-warriors will be looking for the cracks between, incompatible or old versions, and other weak links.

**Meta-happen,** *v.t.* Happen in a simulation or a meta-world.

**Meta-happy,** *adj.* Happy that what just happened did not happen in the real world (perhaps, an explosion, or other bad outcome). Or, happy things are working out right, in a simulation or meta-world.

**Meta-harangue,** *n.* A harangue that could literally go on for a million years, . . . even in wall-clock time.

**Meta-harass,** *v.t.* To use fakes, deep fakes, meta-agents, or some other meta-thing to bother someone.

**Meta-harmless,** *adj.* Probably something that would have been harmful had not all the precautions been taken.

**Meta-hat,** *n.* What you might wear of you have some deep meta-thinking to do.

**Meta-haywire,** *adj.* A metaphor for our time.

## The Metaverse Dictionary

**Meta-hazard,** *n.* That place in your golf simulation where the ball is not supposed to go.

**Meta-history,** *n.* Whatever is in the logs, the archives, and the recordings that stay online, . . . for your convenience. Hunter Thompson once said, "History is hard to know because of all the hired bullshit." And that was before there were serious, organized, world-wide efforts to change history.

**Meta-hitched,** *adj.* "Married" to a meta-world, or the Metaverse. Or, married to someone in a meta-world, a person that you may not be married to in real life.

**Meta-home,** *n.* Where you might be found when you don't seem to be at home.

**Meta-honest,** *adj.* As correct and accurate as you can be amongst all the avatars, fake histories, deep fakes, almost-historical people, simulation, advertizing, creativity, innovation and propaganda.

**Meta-horizontal,** *adj.* Level with respect to other things in the simulation.

**Meta-hunch,** *n.* What thinking might amount to in a simulation or meta-world that conceals many of the meta-facts.

**Meta-hungry,** *adj.* When your avatar thinks that he should be hungry, so he tells you that, . . . as if it is a problem.

**Meta-hurricane,** *n.* A meta-storm that wipes everything out.

**Meta-husband,** *n.* That man you married, but hardly ever see in-person (perhaps because of your meta-jobs). [See Meta-wife.]

# I

**Meta-idea,** *n.* An idea about ideas.

**Meta-identity,** *n.* Any identity that anyone thinks they have, or that another has. Or, a proven identity in a simulation, online game, shopping site, or meta-world. [See Meta-aspect.]

**Meta-ideology,** *n.* An ideology about ideologies that so adequately distinguishes itself from other ideologies about ideologies that one may almost-adhere to it.

**Meta-illuminate,** *adj., v.t.* Without some kind of illumination the Metaverse would be a mostly very dark place. Or, showing figuratively, or without the use of light. Or, revealing of meta-aspects.

**Meta-illusions,** *n.* Perhaps, a tautology.

**Meta-imagine,** *v.* To imagine more freely.

**Meta-imitate,** *v.t.* What happens when you change your settings to "mimic."

**Meta-immune,** *adj.* Immune, because you are not in a real space.

**Meta-imperative,** *n., adj.* Something that just must be that way, in the Metaverse.

**Meta-imprison,** *v.t.* To confine under meta-house arrest, in meta-jail, in meta-prison, or on an external hard drive (and perhaps throwing away the password), in a meta-world.

## The Metaverse Dictionary

**Meta-inadmissible,** *adj.* Currently, dogs and cats and mosquitoes, . . . right out (inadmissible). But, oddly enough, inanimate objects are meta-admissible, as long as they get "the Silicon Valley treatment."

**Meta-income,** *n.* A new line-item on your income tax form: that will appear right after "earned-income" and "investment-income." This is to include all the income generated that accrues to you from the earnings of your avatars and meta-agents, your meta-investments, and possibly income that is associated with the funny things that happen with your funny money. All those things can't possibly go untaxed. [See funny money.]

**Meta-incorporated,** *adj.* A corporation that exists in a meta-world that is legally distinct from a real corporation.

**Meta-independent,** *adj.* Not independent.

**Meta-indicator,** *n.* Something that alerts you in the space that you're in about something that has happened in a space that you are not in.

**Meta-individual,** *n., adj.* Any meta-person. Or, more specifically, a Gary Larson-style cartoon sheep standing on his hind legs singing: "I gotta be me," . . . for real, . . . in a meta-world.

**Meta-indoctrinate,** *v.t.* Teachings for meta-agents (where the subject matter might be considered ideological). Or, teachings for anyone about the Metaverse where the subject matter might be considered ideological. [See Meta-doctrine.]

**Meta-industrialize,** *v.t.* The process of using more and more simulations to assist in industrial processes.

**Meta-ineffective,** *adj.* When a process in some simulation or meta-world is less effective that it might be because there needs to be more association with real-world stuff.

**Meta-inefficiency,** *n.* Trying to get a meta-world process to do what needs doing, when something as simple as hammering a nail in the real world will suffice.

**Meta-inevitable,** *adj.* The future is set.

**Meta-inferior,** *adj.* When or where the meta-world way is deemed to be inferior to the real world way.

**Meta-information,** *n.* Information that is simply not available in the real world.

**Meta-initiative,** *n.* An initiative that is not really a part of practical life most of the time.

**Meta-inland,** *adj.* In the historical-tourism industry, when you are located so far from the meta-water that you are no longer within range for the meta-pirate meta-ship's meta-canons. "Meta-arrgh!" [See Meta-arrgh!]

**Meta-input,** *n.* Everything about the real world, and everything in the real world. Or, everything in a different meta-world.

**Meta-inspect,** *v.t.* Inspect from afar.

**Meta-instrument,** *n.* A meta-scalpel, perhaps. Or, a meta-trombone.

**Meta-interface,** *n.* Perhaps, a virtual interface.

**Meta-interfere,** *v.* Like all those nice helpful phone calls you get all day from strangers and bots, . . . there will probably be a lot more of that kind of thing, . . . for your convenience.

**Meta-intermediary,** *n.* Whoever runs the networks, and the platform you are on.

**Meta-interview,** *n., v.t.* Just answering questions from wherever you are.

**Meta-intimacy,** *n.* Being close from far away. Perhaps, from where it might be safer.

**Meta-invent,** *v.t.* Re-invent something that already exists, but to enable it for the Metaverse. Or, invent something new that would be useless in the real world. Or, to use a simulation to invent something.

**Meta-invest,** *v.t.* Spend a lot of time and/or funny money on something that isn't real. Or, invest in a "Metaverse stock." Or, invest in someone's education.

**Meta-investigate,** *v.t.* To play Inspector Clouseau, or Sherlock Holmes in the Metaverse.

**Meta-invisible,** *adj.* In one of the meta-layers. Or, very small (so small that you miss it). Or, something hiding in plain sight. [See meta-layer.]

**Meta-issue,** *n.* An issue that involves the Metaverse.

# J

**Meta-jail,** *n.* A confining space where your Agent or Avatar can rot, as far as you are concerned, as long as you have other Agents or Avatars.

**Meta-janissary,** *n.* Perhaps, a meta-agent. Perhaps, a human.

**Meta-jewel,** *n.* A jewel made out of software.

**Meta-job,** *n.* A job involving the Metaverse.

**Meta-journalism,** *n.* The collection and editing of news for presentation within a meta-world. Or, the collection and editing of news about the Metaverse for presentation within the Metaverse.

**Meta-journey,** *n.* A trip you take in your mind. Or, a trip you take in a simulation. Or, a trip you take in a meta-world. [See Meta-travel.]

**Meta-judgment,** *n.* An unsure judgment. Or, a judgment that is very sure about meta-stuff.

**Meta-juice,** *n.* The kind of stuff you don't want to spill on your meta-living meta-room meta-rug.

**Meta-jump,** *v.* To jump in a simulation. Or, to jump from one meta-world to another. Or, to consider a jump.

**Meta-jungle,** *n.* An "uncivilized" space in a meta-world. Or, a simulation where there are few rules. Without rules and accountability there is no freedom! Hmmm.

## The Metaverse Dictionary

**Meta-junk,** *n.* Meta-stuff that was previously discarded. Or, meta-stuff that is found to be so little value that it is not worth keeping around.

**Meta-jurisprudence,** *n.* Kinda like jurisprudence in the real world, just way more complicated.

**Meta-jury,** *n.* A jury that is not actually there. Any actual meta-jury member may be pouring over the details of the case (as you might expect), or enjoying their time at Disneyland while occasionally thinking about the case, or they may be any one of a variety of legally-allowable surrogate-jurors or "thumbs up/thumbs down" algorithms (and one that you might trust more than the guy next door anyway).

**Meta-juxtaposition,** *n.* The comparison of things from different meta-worlds.

# K

**Meta-keen,** *adj.* At least seeming to be enthusiastic (as far as you can tell from over there).

**Meta-keep,** *v.t.* Save, stash, or house in a virtual place (as a cloud, or on a drive), especially for the purpose of re-using later.

**Meta-key,** *n., adj.* An important idea or concept that helps with further meta-understanding. Perhaps, something meta-basic. Or, a really hard piece of software that will let you in places. [See Meta-understanding.]

**Meta-keyboard,** *n.* Software that looks like fake hardware, and that plays notes that don't sound like anything unless they are attached to something in the real world.

**Meta-kill,** *v.t.* To stop, and to render helpless and non-operative in a simulation, or in a meta-world.

**Meta-kinky,** *adj.* The type thing that might happen in an augmented reality or virtual reality where meta-gadgets and meta-attachments are involved (and probably where you don't want your parents watching).

**Meta-kit,** *n.* A collection of helpful meta-things.

**Meta-kitty,** *n.* A meta-cat kept as a pet in a simulation or a meta-world. Or, a cartoon kitty for real. Or, a real cat with brain implants connecting it to where you are most of the time, . . . for your convenience.

**Meta-kleptomaniac,** *n.* Someone who goes around stealing things in a law enforcement simulation. Or, someone who goes around stealing things in a meta-world that provides for that kind of optionality. But not someone who goes around stealing things at a shopping site (you know they would not allow that).

**Meta-know,** *v.t.* Know, in a general or high-level sense.

**Meta-knowledge,** *n.* Knowledge about knowledge (like, that it may be good for you, especially in moderation). Or, any knowledge that you might glean from reading the Metaverse How-To Guide.

# L

**Meta-labeled,** *adj.* Tagged in some way. Perhaps a recognition of product placement.

**Meta-labor,** *n.* The labor that is done in a simulation or meta-world. Or, all the labor that is not operations (e.g. "back office" labor, Sales and Marketing, Mergers and Acquisitions, what Senior Management does, all of the out-sourced work, etc.).

**Meta-lag,** *n., v.* The time it takes to set up a simulation. To be taken into account when you are considering whether to use a simulation to help get your product or service to market.

**Meta-landlord,** *n.* A meta-absentee landlord (one that never visits). Or, a landlord in a simulation or meta-world. Or, an owner of a meta-platform.

**Meta-landmark,** *n.* A meta-land mark.

**Meta-language,** *n.* A complete language that is only useful in a meta-world.

**Meta-laugh,** *v.i., n.* The sound of one mouth laughing.

**Meta-launch,** *v.t.* The launch of a meta-platform or simulation, or meta-world.

**Meta-laundry,** *n.* The laundry that meta-people do. There is no getting away from it.

**Meta-law,** *n.* A law that relates to the Metaverse. Perhaps, the whole body of those types of laws. Or, law as it relates to the making and changing of laws.

**Meta-lawful,** *adj.* Something that the powers that be are allowing you to do.

**Meta-lawless,** *adj.* Being creative in a meta-space while at the same time infringing on other people's rights. Or, being destructive in a meta-space.

**Meta-layer,** *n.* While the Metaverse is starting out decentralized and very open to innovation, there are concurrently considerable efforts being made with respect to coordination, standardization, and control. Between the physical layer and the social layer there are many layers that are understood to be there, but that are not so well understood in terms of what roles they play. The various elements can be changed, they are evolving, and are themselves transforming related elements at a fast or not-so-fast rate, depending on the situation. The semi-conductor industry has developed smart chips. Algorithms are everywhere. We already have well-established meta-layers: law, industry regulation, and industry best practices. The world of commercial advertizing can be considered a meta-layer that intermediates itself into many aspects of life. These meta-layers already play a part in the Metaverse, but they are likely to become more connected and linked as time goes on. Manufacturers are going to continually want real-time feedback, and the ability to update and otherwise influence. Other industries working on their own meta-layers: Insurance, Finance, Law Enforcement, and the Censorship and Xxxxxxx industries. You may have already noticed that there are those that control what news you are able to find, what you are able to find with a search, what pops up at you when, and what options you may encounter in your life. [See Meta-.]

**Meta-leadership,** *n.* "Being at the vanguard with respect to Metaverse-related design, technology, science, law, platform development, simulations, etc..

**Meta-leak,** *v.t.* Big or small, this is the kind of thing you want to stop-up immediately.

*The Metaverse Dictionary*

**Meta-learn,** *v.t.* Learn over the internet.

**Meta-lease,** *v.t.* Leasing rather than "owning" your meta-space.

**Meta-leather,** *n.* Probably, lower in quality than meta-vinyl.

**Meta-leave,** *v.t.* You can check out any time you like, but, . . . you can never delete the logs, the audit trail, the backups, the surveillance footage, and any "quasi-permanent" changes that you have made. You can't prevent others from making duplicates or near-duplicates of your stuff, . . . for everyone's convenience. But you can, if you want, start over again as if you were never there.

**Meta-lecture,** *n., v.* Most classes, soon. Maybe there will come a day when a youngster never sees a real human in person until they move from school to the work-force. (Perhaps someone has already invented their own "Meta-brave, new Meta-world.")

**Meta-legacy,** *adj., n.* After someone dies, they may live larger that life for longer than lifetimes (or at least fifteen minutes.) Perhaps Chris Anderson (author of *The Long Tail*) and Almost-Andy Warhol want to fight this one out.

**Meta-leisure,** *n.* Just hanging out in the Metaverse, especially engaging in non-productive activities.

**Meta-letter,** *n.* An email, text, etc..

**Meta-levee,** *n.* The kind of thing that keeps the real world out.

**Meta-library,** *n.* Where you go to read meta-books.

**Meta-life,** *n.* The so-called "good life" of someone, perhaps someone with a desk job.

**Meta-like,** *v.* Like from afar.

**Meta-lingo,** *n.* The language that the meta-locals speak.

## The Metaverse Dictionary

**Meta-living,** *adj., n.* It's a whole new way to live.

**Meta-load,** *n.* A cloud, especially a large, heavy one.

**Meta-limit,** *n.* A perceived limit, given that certain things may stay the meta-same for a while. [See Meta-constant, Clone-limit.]

**Meta-literature,** *n.* Stories and fictional accounts of things happening in the Metaverse.

**Meta-local,** *adj.* Only one or two clicks away.

**Meta-location,** *n.* A meta-place where Meta-movies are made. [See Meta-movie.]

**Meta-log,** *v.t.* An audit log, or chronology of events.

**Meta-look,** *v.t.* Glance at your device. Or, look through your special glasses. Or, to behold a general concept or idea.

**Meta-loose,** *adj.* Not fastened to a particular place in the Metaverse. Perhaps located in a meta-layer.

**Meta-loot,** *v.t., n.* Lots of stolen funny money.

**Meta-lost,** *adj.* Not really lost, it's just that *you* don't know where it is.

**Meta-LPGA ,** *n.* An association for lady golfers who are not very good at golf, or who are very good at Meta-golf. [See Meta-golf.]

**Meta-luggage,** *n.* All of that meta-knowledge that won't fit in your meta-head. Or, all the stuff in your real suitcases that some meta-app can take care of for you.

**Meta-lumber,** *n.* Uncut meta-timber, perhaps near a meta-forest.

**Meta-lurking,** *v.i.* Moving inconspicuously, as viewed by some. But to those in the meta-layers you are just as noticeable and conspicuous as anyone else. [See meta-layer.]

# M

**Meta-made,** *adj.* Made in some simulation or meta-world.

**Meta-male,** *adj.* Anyone (male, female, or a any kind of meta-person).

**Meta-mall,** *n,* Probably a good place to spend your funny money. The feature that allows you to cut-and-paste stores will be much appreciated (by mall owners, and by customers building their own dream mall). The feature that allows you to cut-and-paste meta-sales clerks will also be appreciated.

**Meta-manage,** *v.t.* Manage from a distance, or without being seen (and maybe without even being understood).

**Meta-maneuver,** *n.* A move or positioning that just could not happen in the real world. Or, a maneuver where the meta-person in the highest level (an application) has no chance of being able to figure out what is really going on.

**Meta-manifest,** *adj.* Whatever is manifest to you at your meta-level. [See Meta-level.]

**Meta-manual,** *n.* Probably, most simulations and meta-worlds will come with their own meta-manual. Of course, nobody will read them, just like in the real world.

**Meta-manufacturing,** *n.* Building simulations, online games, shopping sites, meta-world, and meta-platforms.

**Meta-map,** *n.* A map of a meta-world. Or, a map of the Metaverse.

**Meta-marketing,** *n.* Bingo. The raison d'etre of the Metaverse. Hopefully, viral marketing.

**Meta-married,** *adj.* Married in a simulation or meta-world.

**Meta-marshal,** *n.* Anyone in the Metaverse with the powers of a marshal.

**Meta-mart,** *n.* A convenience store in the Metaverse where you buy meta-things with funny money.

**Meta-masculine,** *adj.* Any person or thing that is portraying themselves as being masculine.

**Meta-masquerading,** *v.i.* Pretending to be fake in a different way than usual.

**Meta-master,** *v.t., n.* Anyone who has the power to control a significant part of what happens to you in a simulation, in a meta-world, or on a meta-platform.

**Meta-material,** *adj.* Data, code, or executables (bits and bytes, or whatever comes next).

**Meta-maternity,** *n.* The birthing of little meta-agents.

**Meta-matrix,** *n.* A type of meta-world.

**Meta-matter,** *n.* Hard to define matter. Or, matter that *was* very hard to define. [See Meta-understand.]

**Meta-mature,** *adj.* Experience in the ways that are not so obvious.

**Meta-meal,** *n.* Not the kind your mother used to make.

**Meta-means,** *n.* Possessing the wherewithal to build simulations, meta-worlds, and meta-platforms.

**Meta-measure,** *v.t.* You will need a different kind of tape measure.

## The Metaverse Dictionary

**Meta-mechanics,** *n.* The kind of mechanics that tinker in the meta-platform and the meta-layer levels. Or, a regular mechanic that specializes in meta-cars, and meta-machines in a simulation or meta-world.

**Meta-media,** *n.* Mostly commercials and propaganda, but you might find the odd 3-D sitcom. [See Meta-estate.]

**Meta-mediate,** *v.t.* Connecting and communicating as agent between any or all of the following: simulations, online game, shopping sites, meta-worlds, meta-layers, networks and meta-platforms.

**Meta-Mediterranean,** *n.* A near-duplicate or simulation of a large part of the Earth's surface.

**Meta-meet,** *v.t.* To create a permanent record of your meeting.

**Meta-member,** *n.* A member of an online site. Or, a member of a group that doesn't require membership per se, as with adherents to an ideology (members of the conservative movement, or the ultra-fit).

**Meta-memory,** *n.* Memory that can be photo-realistic and exact, or might be completely wrong. Maybe a deep fake.

**Meta-mend,** *v.t.* To fix or repair something in a simulation or in meta-world, or somewhere else but as it relates to the Metaverse.

**Meta-merchant,** *n.* A business person that buys and sells in the Metaverse.

**Meta-merger,** *n.* A merger of two meta-worlds or two meta-platforms.

**Meta-merit,** *n., v.* Value. Or, value with respect to a higher cause. If something has meta-merit, then it will probably be around for a while.

**Meta-message,** *n.* A message that passes through more filters (and scrutiny) than you could possibly shake a stick at, . . . for everyone's convenience.

**Meta-metaphor,** *n.* After your basic metaphor, going meta-further might be to step on a slippery slope, that might take one to the point of no return. Or, not.

**Meta-method,** *n.* Thinking of something, and then building it out of software and hardware and networks and in clouds and on meta-platforms.

**Meta-mine,** *v.t., n.* To go looking for something in the Metaverse, especially where the finding might be difficult. Or, a deep meta-place. Perhaps, a deep hole with nothing in it but ideas about other stuff.

**Meta-mining,** *v.t.* Figuratively, digging. Or, looking for meta-stuff.

**Meta-minute,** *n.* A unit of time within a simulation or meta-world.

**Meta-mislead,** *v.t.* One way to influence meta-people. Perhaps, the easiest way to make lots of funny money. Use an algorithm, they're lots of fun.

**Meta-misplace,** *v.t.* When you though you left something in one meta-world, when really it was in another meta-world all along.

**Meta-missile,** *n.* Any missile that can go around the world at close to the speed of light is probably a meta-missile and not a real missile. Perhaps, a missile in a military simulation.

**Meta-missing,** *adj.* Something that should be there, but you don't have the right privileges, or you don't have the right settings turned on, or something.

**Meta-mistake,** *n.* The kind of error in a simulation or meta-world that can be backed out, or where you can start over and not make the mistake. Or, a mistake that occurred at a higher level, and you didn't have a chance.

**Meta-misunderstand,** *v.t.* To misunderstand in a way that is probably not your fault. [See Meta-understanding.]

**Meta-misuse,** *v.t.* The name of the game. Or, the meta-name of one particular meta-game.

**Meta-mix,** *v.* A particular collection of bits and bytes.

**Meta-mob,** *n.* A group of meta-people bent on destruction or meta-destruction, or other "undesirable behavior" from someone's perspective.

**Meta-mode,** *n.* Any particular mode one has set within a simulation, online game, shopping site, or meta-world. Perhaps, the mode you need to be in to be able to perceive and interact with the Metaverse in the most efficient way possible.

**Meta-model,** *n.* Aren't we all.

**Meta-modeling,** *v.t.* Wearing clothes that have the designer's name on the outside. Or, pretending to walk up and down fake runways.

**Meta-modern,** *adj.* Something new in a meta-world. In the future it might be hard to find the "modern" stuff because everything from every age will all be mixed together.

**Meta-modify,** *v.t.* Document everything that you are about to do. Make sure you have the proper authorization, and supervision. Make sure the surveillance is operational so that you can't be blamed for something you didn't do. Make a backup copy of everything before you start. Make the update. Make another copy, this time it will be the version of the way you left it. Test your change, and everything that will be affected by your change. Make sure the system logs and audit trail has captured everything. Tell everyone what you did.

## The Metaverse Dictionary

**Meta-momentum,** *n.* A real meta-force that you feel viscerally as everything speeds up.

**Meta-money,** *n.* Funny money. Perhaps block-chain coinage, fiat money, liquid assets, non-fungible tokens, unbreakable meta-bonds, and capital ideas.

**Meta-monist,** *n.* Anyone who thinks there must be some kind of oneness or unity to the Metaverse, even if they find it difficult to get past the dualities and pluralities everywhere.

**Meta-monitor,** *v.t.* Keep an eye on, not from an intense interest, but perhaps because of a fiduciary responsibility.

**Meta-monoculture,** *n.* Where everyone is thinking about doing it. Perhaps, a "melting pot" that is about to explode.

**Meta-monopolize,** *v.t.* Control and dominate from a distance, and in a standoffish way.

**Meta-monopoly,** *n.* A situation where one player dominates a meta-world, the meta-platform industry, or the whole Metaverse.

**Meta-mood,** *n.* A mood that you have in a meta-world. This one single mood might be totally different than the moods that you are having in all the other meta-worlds that you are in, and it might be different than your current real world mood. It's best to just let you avatar deal with it. You avatar may just need a meta-pill, or you avatar may need serious meta-mental meta-therapy.

**Meta-moon,** *n.* Virtually any moon but one orbiting a real planet.

**Meta-moose,** *n.* A moose, in some meta-world.

**Meta-moral,** *n., adj.* A moral that goes beyond, and transcends, and is capable of doing many things that mere mortal-morals can't do.

**Meta-morning,** *n.* A place not a time, and this is wherever it is a morning now.

*The Metaverse Dictionary*

**Meta-movie,** *n.* A movie about a simulation, online game, shopping site, meta-world, network, meta-platform, or the whole Metaverse.

**Meta-mug,** *n.* A coffee mug with an Meta-saying on it. [See Meta-saying.]

**Meta-multitasking,** *n.* Not *seeming* to be doing multiple tasks concurrently, but really doing multiple tasks concurrently (perhaps with the assistance of an avatar, agent, or meta-agent).

**Meta-murder,** *v.t., n.* To delete. Or, to forget about.

# N

**Meta-naked,** *adj.* Appearing to be wearing no clothes, and probably appearing buff or model-like in a simulation, or in a meta-world.

**Meta-name,** *n.* A name that one may use in a simulation or meta-world.

**Metaverse-native,** *adj., n.* An avatar or meta-agent – someone who has always lived in a simulation, meta-world, or elsewhere on a meta-platform.

**Meta-natural,** *adj.* Completely artificial.

**Meta-nature,** *n.* Nature in its symbolic form (clouds indicating rain, bulls indicating stock market rallies). Or, attribute, especially one with an Meta-aspect. Or, Meta-stuff out in the Meta-wild (on a nature trail).

**Meta-near,** *adv., adj., prep.* Within range.

**Meta-need,** *n.* The need for things like meaning and purpose. Or, the need for more meta-stuff (like fake air, water, food, shelter, clothing, and fake basic cable).

**Meta-nerd,** *n.* A person that you will probably never meet in the real world.

**Meta-network,** *n., v.* The network that the network is in.

**Meta-networking,** *v.t.* Meeting meta-people.

## The Metaverse Dictionary

**Meta-new,** *adj.* Used, but in very good condition (and it will stay that way forever unless someone makes an update to it).

**Meta-news,** *n.* A news message from or about a meta-world. Or, news about the news, the press, or the media itself.

**Meta-niche,** *n.* Some may be easy to figure out, but many not.

**Meta-night,** *n.* A place not a time, and this is wherever it is a morning now. [See Meta-zone.]

**Meta-nimble,** *adj.* Able to move about in the Metaverse like nobody's business.

**Meta-noise,** *n.* Irrelevant or meaningless data occurring along with desired information.

**Meta-normal,** *adj., n.* Probably, not very normal at all.

**Meta-normative,** *adj.* The "real world" is still has a certain pull, in both design and understanding, and so will exert it's own kind of gravity.

**Meta-north,** *adv., adj.* Like the North Star, or magnetic north, but a little bit more like a Hollywood Star.

**Meta-nosedive,** *n.* A nosedive does not always mean a crash, unlike before.

**Meta-nothing,** *n.* Something, signifying nothing.

**Meta-noticeable,** *adj.* A phenomenon, in a simulation, online game, shopping site, or meta-world.

**Meta-nuisance,** *n.* Almost everybody else. Especially company's that advertise.

*The Metaverse Dictionary*

**Meta-nurse,** *n.* A nurse practiced in the art of caring for meta-people. Or, a nurse that is really somewhere else. Or, a nurse in a simulation.

**Meta-nut,** *n.* Someone that gets carried away, in the Metaverse. (For some reason, a disproportionately high percentage of electrical engineers seem to be Meta-nut cases.)

# O

**Meta-obedience,** *n.* Adherence to the rules of a simulation or meta-world. In some simulations or meta-worlds, meta-obedience might be desirable or required, and in others meta-disobedience might be encouraged or essential. Or, obedience to a higher principle that is also at play in the situation.

**Meta-obfuscate,** *v.t.* To hide something from view in the Metaverse, perhaps in a meta-layer. Or, to muddle or complexify an ideology, not just a particular message. [See Meta-layer.]

**Meta-obscene,** *adj.* Perhaps, the real world.

**Meta-observation,** *n.* Something being noticed without the noticing being noticed. Or, the noticing of something beyond. [See meta-beyond.]

**Meta-obsolete,** *adj.* Archived. Or, still around only because so many people wrote about the subject over the years.

**Meta-obstacle,** *n.* A boundary, within the Metaverse. Or, an impediment to thought.

**Meta-ocean,** *n.* A very large amount of meta-water located on top of (as it were) the otherwise "dry" meta-land of a meta-world. Or, a near-duplicate or simulation of a large body of water.

**Meta-oceangoing,** *adj.* Of a meta-ship for meta-travelling on meta-oceans. You might want to take a meta-book for the meta-journey.

**Meta-offence,** *n.* Probably an offence that can be backed out.

## The Metaverse Dictionary

**Meta-office,** *n.* It would be both prudent and meta-prudent to have both an office in the real world, and a meta-office in some quiet meta-space.

**Meta-officer,** *n.* An officer in a meta-army in some meta-world.

**Meta-official,** *n., adj.* An official in a meta-world. Or, an official speaking for a meta-world.

**Meta-ogling,** *v.* Depending on your privileges, settings, and inclinations, what you might be able to do surreptitiously from a "lower" meta-level.

**Meta-oil,** *n.* Metaphorically, how you get rich in a meta-world.

**Meta-operation,** *n.* A procedure that medical students and surgeons do to stay in practice so that they don't botch your operation (probably in a simulation).

**Meta-opponent,** *n.* The thing that looks like a tennis player that seems to be right in front of you over there. That's it, your "swing" button is just to your left.

**Meta-option,** *n.* Perhaps, a selection from a menu. Or, a choices that arrive at the very most inconvenient of times (probably advertising, or a misdirection). Or, the option to consider your choices from a more general perspective.

**Meta-organization,** *n.* An organization not working on anything specific enough for for it to be a Meta-company.

**Meta-original,** *adj.* Perhaps, the real-world version.

**Meta-originate,** *v.t.* Cobble together. [See Meta-create, Meta-credit, Meta-make.]

**Meta-outfit,** *n.* Perhaps, something that looks like a real outfit.

**Meta-outlaw,** *n.*  Someone who is not only looking for trouble in the Metaverse, but who has actually found some. Or, someone who thinks so far out-of-the-box that they really need to be careful defining their terms.

**Meta-output,** *n.*  Output from above, as it were.

**Meta-outsider,** *n.*  A real person.

**Meta-outsource,** *v.t.*  When your avatar hires a meta-agent.

**Meta-overlap,** *v.t.*  What happens when simulations, online games, shopping sites, or meta-worlds collide. Or, the overlaps of two or more ideas. Or, the overlap of two or more ideologies. Or, the overlap of two or more generalizations.

# P

**Meta-pace,** *n., v.* A pace that might be much faster than desirable. Often, the pace set by those working 24 x 7.

**Meta-pajamas,** *n.* Whatever you wearing, when your sleepwear is visible from the Metaverse.

**Meta-palpable,** *adj.* Those parts of the Metaverse are perceptible, clear, and perhaps tangible.

**Meta-paper,** *n.* Fake paper. The "meta-paperless meta-office" is still years away.

**Meta-par,** *n.* A setting on your meta-club, in meta-golf.

**Meta-paradigm,** *n.* A considered and structured way of thinking about paradigms. (Popularized by Thomas Kuhn.) [See Meta-aspect.]

**Meta-park,** *n.* A simulation of a civilized jungle, perhaps one where the amount of time spent feeding the meta-birds is maximized.

**Meta-part,** *n.* That part of something that is connected to a simulation, online game, shopping site, or meta-world.

**Meta-participating,** *v.* Living on planet Earth.

**Meta-particles,** *n.* Words.

**Meta-party,** *v.i.* Probably, the party all the avatars and meta-agents are going to vote for.

**Meta-passport,** *n.* What you use to help get yourself from one meta-place to another.

**Meta-password,** *n.* "Meta-rover," or "Meta-Amazon," or "Meta-password."

**Meta-past,** *adj., prep., n.* Whatever ends up on those storage devices.

**Meta-patent,** *n.* A patent for some unique component of the Metaverse. Or, a patent secured within a meta-world or legal system simulation.

**Meta-patient,** *n.* A patent in your hospital simulation. Probably that guy "pulling the cord" (pressing the button, or clicking) for a nurse right now.

**Meta-pay,** *v.t.* To exchange funny money for serious stuff. Or, to exchange fake money for fake stuff.

**Meta-payment,** *n.* Data. Unlike real inanimate things (like cash) that decay over time, meta-payments never stop being copied from storage device to backup storage device, and perhaps becoming more important themselves as linked meta-people or meta-events become more important over time.

**Meta-people,** *n.* See Meta-person.

**Meta-perceptible,** *adj.* Perceptible in or from the Metaverse.

**Meta-permit,** *n.* To do or not to do, that is the question. Whether 'tis nobler in the mind to get a permit, and then trigger all kinds of scrutiny and all kinds of information going this way and that, . . . or to just sit still and do nothing.

**Meta-persnickety,** *adj.* Recognizing that simulations often require great precision just to work.

**Meta-person,** *n.* Any "sentient" being that has some significant Metaverse presence. Or, any "smart" being that has some significant Metaverse presence, especially one capable of replacing a human or taking a job away from a human (to possibly include an "AI," "robot," "bot," "smart car," "agent," "meta-agent," "avatar," or "meta-avatar").

**Meta-personal,** *adj.* "It's never just about you anymore. It's about everyone like you. You are but a symbol. It's about what you represent. One must put on one's Meta-hat, as it was. This must be seen as a "big-picture" issue and from the almost-impersonal and hyper-generalized perspective. Now that we've transcended your experience, you can just crawl away, and leave us alone, . . . to now, . . . discuss something completely different." "Did you have a good time?" "Ok, where are the logs." "See, there, that's what I've been talking about."

**Meta-personality,** *n.* One you probably won't recognize. Maybe, one who doesn't recognize you. [See Meta-person.]

**Meta-personnel,** *n.* Gaggles of bots or meta-agents.

**Meta-perspective,** *n.* This one, generally speaking. (Any one of the perspective presented in this here Meta-Dictionary.)

**Meta-PGA,** *n.* An association for golfers who either like practicing before a game, or who are very good at Meta-golf. [See Meta-golf.]

**Meta-phase(s),** *n.* There used to just be a few: gas, liquid, solid, plasma, and Bose-Einstein concentrate. Now, many more are bound to be invented and used. Or, the phase after: Analysis, Design, Build, Paperwork, and Artificial Deadline.

**Meta-phobia,** *n.* The fear of ideas and generalities.

**Metaphor,** *n.* Referring to one kind of thing instead of another to suggest a likeness or analogy between them.

**Meta-physical,** *adj.* Fake stuff that exhibits properties of real stuff.

*The Metaverse Dictionary*

**Meta-picture,** *n.* A picture of a picture. The movie My Cousin Vinny (1992) is a meta-picture in that it is a picture about a picture of tire skid-marks.

**Meta-pinch,** *v.t., n.* When a meta-man reaches over to tweak a meta-woman's backside, and then you hear a sounds like Harpo's horn.

**Meta-pint,** *n.* Slightly less than a full pint, because of the space that needs to be left for the advertizing at the top.

**Meta-piracy,** *n.* Having a good time, especially stealing other meta-people's funny doubloons.

**Meta-place,** *n.* Any place in a simulation or meta-world.

**Meta-platform,** *n.* Internet infrastructure, that includes hardware, software, and network components and that might be used to support such things as simulations, online games, shopping sites, and meta-worlds.

**Meta-police,** *v.t.* The kind of police that you cant see coming. Those keeping the Metaverse safe, . . . for everyone's convenience. Or, those who might guard the full spectrum of thought.

**Meta-porn,** *n.* Sometimes, almost as good as real porn.

**Meta-position,** *n.* The coordinates of a position within a simulation.

**Meta-possible,** *adj.* If you can think it, like you can think of flying, it will probably be much easier to accomplish in a meta-world. Flying is still difficult in the real world.

**Meta-power,** *n.* The power that comes with of supervening, surveillance, and control at every level.

**Meta-powerful,** *adj.* Well-connected (same as always).

**Meta-practical,** *adj.* To behave in ways fitting for the circumstances, even though what you are actually doing might seem ludicrous.

## The Metaverse Dictionary

**Meta-practice,** *v.* The use of simulations potentially allow for practicing and experimenting in a less expensive way (as measured in time and resources, and after the initial setup is done).

**Meta-predicament,** *n.* Not being able to find your way out of a simulation or meta-world.

**Meta-predict,** *v.t.* To predict with greater accuracy because of the increased knowledge or control that come with your privileges in a simulation or meta-world.

**Meta-prefab,** *adj., n.* Template materials from which future prefabricated things might be made.

**Meta-present,** *adj., n.* The time, which might not be the same as wall-clock time, and can be set to be different in different simulations or meta-worlds.

**Meta-private,** *adj.* There is no such thing. [See "private" in a real dictionary.]

**Meta-procedure,** *n.* A procedure that refers to things in such a general way that it is of little practical use, even though it may have theoretical or hypothetical use.

**Meta-process,** *n.* A process in a simulation.

**Meta-produce,** *v.* Supervise.

**Meta-product,** *n.* The almost-opposite of a meta-service in a meta-world. Or, the actual service that is being provided in a simulation.

**Meta-productive,** *adj.* Probably, at least as productive as one would be in the real world. Maybe, many more times as productive as one would be in a the real world.

## The Metaverse Dictionary

**Meta-profession,** *n.* One's profession in a simulation, or in a meta-world. This profession may or may not be the same as that person's profession in a different environment, or in the real world. Meta-professions may or may not rely as heavily on certifications. Or, a professional working in a Meta-field. [See Meta-field.]

**Meta-programmer,** *n.* Anyone in the Metaverse that is programming the real world, . . . for fun and profit, . . . and for everyone's convenience.

**Meta-psychology,** *n.* The study of the study of brains. [See Meta-therapy, Meta-think.]

**Meta-pub,** *n.* A place where meta-people go to practice their meta-drinking, their meta-socializing, and their meta-darts. Also, a place for high-intensity meta-tagging.

**Meta-puzzle,** *n., v.* When our universe is expanding faster, those born will have no way of knowing about other galaxies. Likewise, in a meta-world, one might never be able to have all the facts and map cause to effect (simply because with one's settings and privileges one is denied or missing important details).

# Q

**Meta-qualified,** *adj.* Trained, and with the meta-certificate files to prove it.

**Meta-quality,** *adj., n.* The quality of "being made out of technology." Or, valuable meta-stuff. Or, only those ideas, abstractions, and generalities that are elegant, fashionable, or highfalutin.

**Meta-quantity,** *n.* A quantity in a simulation.

**Meta-quarry,** *n.* Anything in a hunting simulation, except maybe the meta-trees and the meta-rocks.

**Meta-question,** *v.t., n.* The kind of question for which many different answers, and many different perspectives might be relevant and important.

**Meta-questionnaire,** *n.* A comprehensive questionnaire that asks about your simulation experience. Or, a questionnaire that asks about your meta-world experience.

**Meta-quorum,** *n.* Having at least the right number of meta-people to be able to start. Or, having at least the right number of generalizations, abstractions, and nifty new ideas to be able to start.

**Meta-quota,** *n.* Having at least the acceptable share or proportion of meta-stuff in each category or division.

**Meta-quote,** *v.t., n.* A quote about meta-stuff, a meta-person, a simulation, online game, shopping site, meta-world, meta-platform, or the Metaverse.

# R

**Meta-rain,** *n.* Rain that is not wet.

**Meta-rare,** *adj.* So rare that there is, perhaps, less than a billion things like it. [See clone-limit.]

**Meta-recordings,** *n.* Online business meetings and other things that Big Tech companies just stash away, . . . for your convenience. Or, online training materials. Or, online entertainment.

**Meta-recover,** *v.t.* To go back in a simulation to a meta-time when the problem has not yet occurred.

**Meta-redundancy,** *n.* The whole point of simulations.

**Meta-regret,** *v.i.* "Regrets, I've had a few. But then again, too few to mention." "But, generally speaking, bad things happened whenever I did these types of things: drinking too much, . . . ."

**Meta-relationship,** *n.* The kind of relationship that is probably no so close when you measure it in feet and inches. [See Meta-friends.]

**Meta-remark,** *n.* A remark that might make it into a meta-balloon comment, as long as it's brief.

**Meta-repair,** *v.t.* To fix something fake. Or, to fix something general in nature.

**Meta-replace,** *v.t.* Run the simulation over again, and this time try Clarke Gable, Vivien Leigh and yourself in the starring roles.

**Meta-result,** *n.* The result, or combination of many results from a given simulation.

**Meta-retail,** *adj.* Wholesale.

**Meta-rights,** *n.* Those privileges that you think are yours until someone takes them away.

**Meta-risk,** *n.* What you get a lot of when the simulation or meta-world has no safety net. Or, what you might get if the menu that you are looking at does not list a "Plan B." Or, what might go up after some meta-agent has just told you that he has "an angle."

**Meta-robot,** *n.* A software robot.

**Meta-rocket,** *n.* Some thing that goes up, up, and away, . . . figuratively speaking.

**Meta-role,** *n.* Being "left right out," . . . for example. Or, "one the sidelines."

**Meta-room,** *n.* Just a walk-in closet, until you get a bigger house.

**Meta-rope,** *n.* The kind of rope that can stretch across a meta-abyss no problem. (There you go, Mr. Nietzsche.)

**Meta-route,** *n.* Perhaps, a detour over or around some treacherous software.

**Meta-routine,** *n* Get up, think about something wise, then think about something abstract that is also gargantuan, and then have breakfast.

**Meta-rule,** *n.* Rule of thumb. Or, principle.

**Meta-ruler,** *n.* Perhaps, a ruler used to test the validity of Euclid's fifth axiom.

**Meta-run,** *v.i.* Run, on exercise equipment that is connected to the internets. Or, run in a simulator. Or, to figuratively run away from something.

**Meta-runway,** *n.* A meta-walkway, in a simulation or meta-world. Especially one used by aspiring "meta-models" who wants to show off their meta-outfits. Or, that part of the meta-airport in a meta-world where meta-planes get together to sniff each other's butts before taking off on a long trip.

# S

**Meta-safe,** *adj.* Safe, . . . given that all of the various stakeholders have some legal justification for being able to see, listen, know, and often to some limited degree control what you know and do, . . . for everyone else's safety and convenience. No person or thing is completely safe, the best you can hope for is meta-safety.

**Meta-salary,** *n.* Whatever a meta-agent working at arm's length gets these days.

**Meta-sale,** *n.* A sale that happens in a meta-world, or a sale that happens elsewhere in the Metaverse. Or, a sale of a meta-world, or a meta-platform. Or, a sale of something that is not done in-person (or "in-thing," if both the buyer and seller are non-sentient robots).

**Meta-saloon,** *n.* Probably, where meta-agents hang out when off duty — due to their programming (and the meta-laws that preventing them form going completely haywire). Or, a mostly-real saloon sporting Metaverse connectivity, . . . for their patron's convenience. (You employees might be there right now.)

**Meta-sanity,** *n.* Perhaps, something to be guarded.

**Meta-satellite,** *n.* A communications device in orbit around a planet. Or, a communications device, the movements of which are being simulated.

**Meta-savvy,** *adj.* Skill in dealing with meta-stuff.

*The Metaverse Dictionary*

**Meta-scale,** *n.* A scale, in a simulation.

**Meta-scarce,** *adj.* Something that cannot be readily copied with the "copy" command.

**Meta-scare,** *n.* A scare that can be ignored or turned off. Or, a scare that cannot be ignored or turned off.

**Meta-scene,** *n.* What you think you see.

**Meta-schedule,** *n.* A schedule in a simulation.

**Meta-scoop,** *n.* A dollop of news that is dished out by anyone to anyone quickly and before anyone else finds out.

**Meta-screwball,** *adj.* Being amiably unpredictable in the Metaverse.

**Meta-script,** *n.* A script that goes all over the place.

**Meta-scrutinize,** *v.t.* To consider from the thirty-thousand foot level. Or, to consider the details in a simulation or meta-world.

**Meta-seamless,** *adj.* Barely noticeable. The ideal for transitions between meta-worlds is that they are as meta-seamless as possible.

**Meta-search,** *v.t.* Type or talk, . . . and then look.

**Meta-season,** *n.* A season experienced from afar. One thing about a a Metaverse is Winter, Spring, Summer, and Fall all simultaneously. Or, a season that someone invented just for their meta-world. Or, a time to think big and important thoughts.

**Meta-sex,** *n.* Any of the various kinds of intimate relations that do not produce children, and especially those that produce network traffic logs, audit logs, surveillance footage, pictures, sound recordings, 3-D images, and feature length films (all of which may never be available to you).

## The Metaverse Dictionary

**Meta-shirt,** *n.* Any shirt that has a meta-saying on it. [See Meta-saying.]

**Meta-shopkeeper,** *n.* Whoever the sales clerk bot or meta-agent reports to.

**Meta-shopper,** *n.* The best kind. One that you don't need to schmooze.

**Meta-ski,** *v.* In a skiing in a simulation, especially when learning how to ski, or when it's not winter where you are.

**Meta-sky,** *n.* That huge volume of meta-air underneath the meta-blue at the meta-top.

**Meta-slang,** *n.* Words or phrases that apply to a simulation, online game, shopping site, meta-world, or meta-platform; especially ones that are new and used informally.

**Meta-smile,** *v., n.* The happy-face emoji. Or, a smiling avatar.

**Meta-snow,** *n.* The fake white flakes that fall when you turn a meta-world upside down.

**Meta-sociology,** *n.* The study of the meta-aspects of meta-people in groups. [See Meta-people.]

**Meta-solution,** *adj., n.* Years ago, according to Homer Simpson, beer was the cause of, and the solution to all of life's problems. Then the Internet became the cause of and the solution to all of life's problems. Now, the Metaverse promises some very attractive solutions to many of life's problems that until now we didn't know we would have.

**Meta-sound,** *adj.* A sound in a simulation or meta-world.

**Meta-speak,** *n., v.* The kind of language, spoken or written, that includes meta-words, especially paragraphs, whole texts, or orations

## The Metaverse Dictionary

made using a relatively high percentage of meta-words. [See Meta-word, Meta-expression, Meta-angle, Meta-aspect, Meta-method, Meta-principle, Meta-something, Meta-stuff, Meta-think.]

**Meta-speculation,** *n.* A considered or an educated guess about the Metaverse.

**Meta-speech,** *n.* The lingo peculiar to a meta-world. [See Meta-speak.]

**Meta-sponsored,** *adj.* Love of the Metaverse is a many-sponsored Meta-thing.

**Meta-spot,** *n.* Dot. Or, pixel.

**Meta-staff,** *n.* Meta-people that work for you. [See Meta-employee.]

**Meta-star,** *n.* A meta-person that many meta-people have on their meta-radar.

**Meta-start,** *v.* Perhaps, the meta-button on the bottom left.

**Meta-stop,** *v.t.* To stop a simulation, perhaps with the intent of restarting it. Or, to position oneself as stationary relative to something that is beyond, after, supporting, or transcending you.

**Meta-storage,** *n.* That part of a meta-world that is so full of meta-junk in meta-boxes piled meta-sky high that almost-nobody ever searches it with keyboard commands.

**Meta-store,** *n.* An Meta-place online where you can really buy meta-stuff. [See Meta-world.]

**Meta-storm,** *n.* Perhaps, when it's a blustery day in your simulation.

**Meta-story,** *n.* A story that starts like this: "Once upon a time there was a meta-world, and . . ." And it might end like this: ". . . and they lived quite happily, until . . . one day . . . [and that goes straight into the next meta-story. [You will need to hit the "ESC" button or make some weird gesture to meta-actually get meta-out.]

**Meta-strange,** *adj.* Unconventional, in a real sense.

**Meta-stranger,** *n.* Anyone you meet that is not surrounded by meta-tags. [See Meta-tags]

**Meta-strategy,** *n.* A strategy about strategizing itself.

**Meta-stream,** *n., v.* Probably something impressive that is happening in real-time.

**Meta-street,** *n.* A street in a simulation or a meta-world. Or, *the* street we are all on.

**Meta-strength,** *n.* A variable in a simulation. Or, a variable in a meta-level or meta-platform.

**Meta-stress,** *n.* Psychological tension that is difficult to measure accurately and separately from other stressors because the root cause is the Metaverse that is all around us.

**Meta-strip,** *v.i.* To take off your avatar's clothes.

**Meta-structure,** *n.* The basis for a structure. Perhaps, a frame.

**Meta-stuff,** *n.* Any meta-thing in a simulation, online game, shopping site, meta-world, or meta-platform. Anything made out of meta-matter, meta-energy, meta-substance, or other meta-abstract thing. Or, anything that has meta-aspects. [See Meta-aspect, Meta-abstract, Meta-thing.]

**Meta-stunt,** *n.* A trick that would probably be impossible in the real world. Perhaps, one meant to attract attention or publicity.

**Meta-substance,** *n.* That which would meta-be by definition. Or, a hard to define substance. Any of the real fake substances. [See Meta-abstract, Meta-real, Meta-thing, Meta-stuff, and a recent edition of the Handbook of Chemistry and Physics to see what is definitely not not just a meta-substance.]

**Meta-sun,** *n.* That single star in the sky that you can see from many angles at once Earth simultaneously.

**Meta-sunlight,** *n.* That which exposes or makes clear those meta-things that add to social and mental insight.

**Meta-super,** *adj.* Able to do super-human things because of a feature of the Metaverse. [See Meta-hero.]

**Meta-surrogate,** *v.t., n.* To act on behalf of another in the Metaverse.

**Meta-sustain,** *v.t.* To keep a meta-world going. Or, to keep the Metaverse going.

**Meta-swear,** *v.* To use the word "meta" as a four-letter word.

**Meta-system,** *n.* What a simulation, an online game, a shopping site, a meta-world, and a meta-platform are.

# T

**Meta-tangible,** *adj., n.* Meta-things that are not abstract.

**Meta-tangle,** *n.* Any complex or convoluted mess of links in the Metaverse.

**Meta-tank,** *n.* Smart and connected sport-utility vehicle (SUV).

**Meta-tantamount,** *adj.* Nearly equivalent in value, significance, or effect to something in the real world.

**Meta-tax,** *n.* What every government and meta-government wants. Could be even more lucrative than the taxes on cigarettes and booze.

**Meta-team,** *v.t., n.* Those people you work with that you have never met.

**Meta-technical,** *adj.* Mostly, something easy enough that a child could do it. Partly, something so complicated that only an expert can figure it out.

**Meta-teleprompter,** *n.* A teleprompter that the audience can't see from their vantage point.

**Meta-tenant,** *n.* Whoever rents a place on a meta-platform for their simulation, online game, shopping site, or meta-world.

**Meta-tennis,** *n.* The very best part of the Metaverse.

**Meta-terminology,** *n.* What you are looking at now.

**Meta-test,** *n.* A test in a simulation environment.

## The Metaverse Dictionary

**Meta-theft,** *n.* The theft of funny money. Or the theft of a thing in a simulation, computer game, shopping site, or meta-world.

**Meta-theory,** *n.* A theory about theories.

**Meta-there,** *adv., n.* Somewhere, but you really don't know where.

**Meta-thing,** *n.* A thing in a simulation, online game, shopping site, or meta-world. Or, a concept, idea, generalization, or abstraction (something that a brain does).

**Meta-think,** *v.* To think about concepts, ideas, generalizations, or abstractions. [See Meta-method, Meta-therapy, Meta-way.]

**Meta-time,** *n.* The time in your simulation. Or, in the real-world, the space-time continuum governs, and time runs slightly slower up where the satellites are. So you figure it out.
[See Meta-travel.]

**Meta-toilet,** *n.* A potty, specifically one that is connected and smart.

**Meta-tool,** *n.* A handy software feature designed to fix or adjust something.

**Meta-trace,** *v., n.* To follow directly, or with the aid of an audit trail, at least as far as the first brain that you get to that can change it's own mind.

**Meta-transit,** *v.t.* Busses and trains that are connected and smart.

**Meta-transition,** *n.* A transition from one simulation, online game, shopping site, or meta-world to another.

**Meta-translation,** *n.* Translations that happen for you automatically. You will never need to learn another language again. [See Douglas Adams' H2G2 series regarding babel fish.]

**Meta-transport,** *v.t., n.* Smart vehicles. [See Meta-tour, Meta-travel.]

*The Metaverse Dictionary*

**Meta-travel,** *v., n.* Not going the regular way.

**Meta-trick,** *n., v.t.* A not-so-obvious helpful a-ha of understanding.

**Meta-trifle,** *n.* Not such a big deal in the grand scheme of profound thought.

**Meta-trip,** *v., n.* A trip that can be over in a jiffy.

**Meta-troglodyte,** *n.* A meta-person characterized by reclusive habits, especially when in meta-worlds.

**Meta-trouble,** *n.* Serious trouble.

**Meta-trucking,** *n.* Tons of stuff moving around in the real world with no human behind the wheel. (What could possibly go wrong?)

**Meta-true,** *adj., adv.* True in a simulation, online game, shopping site, or meta-world. [See Meta-understanding.]

**Meta-trustworthy,** *adj.* As trustworthy as the environment allows.

**Meta-turn,** *v.* Any figurative turn, or metaphorical turn.

**Meta-twin,** *n.* Look-alike. Doppelganger.

**Meta-type,** *n., v.* Maybe a type that you've never heard of before. Or, when one types using the letters of a keyboard in a meta-world.

# U

**Meta-ubiquity,** *n.* Ubiquity, interoperability, standards, quality, and security are going to be struggling with creativity, opportunity, independence, competition, uniqueness, and speed-to-market.

**Meta-ugly,** *adj.* Something that takes a little getting used to, because it has a software-determined form. Or, something that takes a little getting used to, because it doesn't have a physical form.

**Meta-umpire,** *n.* Somebody has got to make a judgment call now and then about the multiple directions the Metaverse goes in; but, we'll probably just leave that up to the Metaverse itself, . . . for the convenience of all the stakeholders, and stakeholder Earth.

**Meta-unbalanced,** *adj.* Probably, self-balancing. Or, Meta-weird.

**Meta-underfund,** *v.t.* To under-fund only to the extent that the real-world version needs more support.

**Meta-understanding,** *n.* An understanding of meta-things. Or, an understanding that goes beyond things and meta-things. [See Meta-things.]

**Meta-underworld,** *n.* An informal reference to the meta-layers beneath the layer you happen to be in. Or, of those parts of the world of organized crime that might involve or operate in parts of the Metaverse.

**Meta-unemployed,** *adj.* All of those non-human meta-people that are out of work because their human counterparts still have their jobs. [See meta-people.]

**Meta-unexpected,** *adj.* One of the most-used slang exclamations: "Meta-unexpected!" in reference to surprise happenings that are at least in-part caused by something in the Metaverse.

**Meta-unfair,** *adj.* Our world is already not fair, but when things are not fair because of something about the Metaverse then they can be said to be meta-unfair.

**Meta-unfinished,** *adj.* Like the Internet, the Metaverse will never be finished, it will just keep evolving.

**Meta-unfit,** *adj.* Perhaps, fit in the real world, but not fit for a particular meta-world, or the Metaverse.

**Meta-unstable,** *adj.* Instability might become the chief problem introduced by the ever growing Metaverse.

**Meta-unusual,** *adj.* As of this writing Meta-speak might be considered meta-unusual. Many things in the Metaverse will probably be considered unusual, at least at first. [See Meta-speak.]

**Meta-update,** *v.t., n.* Not just a regular update, but a meta-update.

**Meta-utility,** *adj.* A utility that delivers or operates in a meta-environment.

# V

**Meta-vacant,** *adj.* Unoccupied; for example, as a simulation, online game, shopping site, or meta-world might be before they open their meta-doors for the first time.

**Meta-vacation,** *n.* Any vacation from work when you don't leave home to visit somewhere special.

**Meta-vacuum,** *n.* A meta-world with so much unused meta-space that it could cause a type of suffocation, or at least boredom.

**Meta-valuable,** *adj.* Something of value in the Metaverse that might not be nearly as valuable elsewhere.

**Meta-value,** *v.t.* The actual value of something that is meta-valuable. Or, the value of concepts, ideas, learning, and an education.

**Meta-variable,** *n.* A container of a data-value where if that were changed then something else would change in a meta-environment. [See Meta-constant.]

**Meta-variety,** *n.* More variety than that to which you might be accustomed. Evolution has relied on variety and competition, but it has not ever seen the kind of variety and competition that will exist in the Metaverse.

**Meta-niche,** *n.* A place of relative stability amidst the kind of competition and market forces elsewhere, . . . for as long as it can be defended.

**Meta-vault,** *n.* A location online allowing less access than most other places.

**Meta-vehicle,** *n.* Autonomous vehicles. Or, a clever way to move generalities around. Or, a vehicle that is perhaps *way* more advanced than mere so-called "smart" cars.

**Meta-venture,** *n.* To venture out into the new frontier.

**Meta-verbiage,** *n.* Lots of Meta-speak. Or, lots of legalese about generalities and the behavior of meta-people. "First-born screen" kinda stuff.

**Meta-verify,** *v.t.* To check that something is ok, possibly by using a simulation first.

**Meta-versatile,** *adj.* Virtually endlessly modifiable.

**Meta-version,** *n.* Probably, the smart version of something. Or, the version of your simulation. Or, the version of your online game, or meta-world.

**Meta-vertical,** *adj.* Not leaning over, but not necessarily at right angles with, or parallel to anything.

**Meta-viable,** *adj.* Supported by meta-layers.

**Meta-vicinity,** *n.* Perhaps, right next door, in a meta-world. Or, close, like near-cognates are close.

**Meta-view,** *n.* The view you have, not from your windows, but from your computer, and straight through to other people's living rooms.

**Meta-voice,** *n.* Not your real voice, but one of the other voices you have.

**Meta-vote,** *v.* Whatever might happen when a meta-person clicks on something, perhaps with their feet.

**Meta-voyage,** *n.* When you read about a voyage, or view pictures of places. Meta-voyages are safer, and Meta-travel generally is a lot less time-consuming than real travel. [See Meta-travel.]

*The Metaverse Dictionary*

**Meta-vulnerable,** *adj.* Capable of being deleted or taken down at any moment. Or, capable of being disagreed with, perhaps by someone with better ideas.

# W

**Meta-wage,** *n.* Perhaps, less than the minimum wage. A lot might depend on whether smart things and bots get into "collective bargaining," or whether they figure out a way around the need to do that.

**Meta-wait,** *v.i.* The Metaverse waits for no one. However, within a particular meta-world there might be rules about "appropriate input" ( like the length of your new password), and then . . . it will wait forever if necessary.

**Meta-waiter,** *n.* The meta-person that pushes the button that gets your food to your table.

**Meta-waitress,** *n.* See Meta-waiter.

**Meta-walk,** *v.i.* The kind of walk that you avatar might have. Perhaps, one of Monty Python's silly walks.

**Meta-want,** *v.t.* Want, but only if you can order it from home.

**Meta-wanted,** *adj.* "Wanted, one good bot. Apply within. You need a meta-shirt and meta-shoes to enter here."

**Meta-war,** *n.* A sneaky one. [See Meta-method, Meta-way.]

**Meta-warehouse,** *n.* Perhaps, a small data storage device containing gazillions of meta-things just waiting to be meta-used.

**Meta-warped,** *adj.* Twisted enough to be dangerous.

## The Metaverse Dictionary

**Meta-warrantee,** *n.* An assurance by a manufacturing company that will last until the meta-thing pops out of existence.

**Meta-waste,** *n.* Anything extra. Or, bad ideas.

**Meta-wasteful,** *adj.* What happens when getting something done quickly is more important than getting it done economically.

**Meta-watch,** *v.t.* Watch from your computer screen or mobile device.

**Meta-waves,** *n.* Software functions, Or, arrangements of data particles. Or, what your meta-friend does as they meta-leave.

**Meta-way,** *n.* A way that is enhance with, or plagued by so many options that it would be almost-impossible to start talking about this.

**Meta-weak,** *adj.* Less strong than other meta-things, but still subject to settings and options, and meta-settings and meta-options, and meta-meta-settings and meta-meta-options, . . . etcetera.

**Meta-wealthy,** *adj.* Perhaps, possessing lots of funny money.

**Meta-wear,** *v., n.* Put on (like a nametag). Or, tie around the waist over your clothes. Or, Meta-shirts or other clothing with Meta-sayings on them. [See Meta-sayings, Meta-season, Meta-shirts.]

**Meta-weather,** *n.* Perhaps, sunlight that wipes out some of the data around you, rain that is not wet, snowflakes that fall up and that talk a mile a minute, wind that pushes everything away from you in every direction, indoor storms, and clouds that contain worlds.

**Meta-wedding,** *n.* A wedding rehearsal, perhaps. Or, a wedding simulation.

**Meta-weekend,** *n.* With all the pressure to get things done as quickly as possible these days, a meta-weekend might be a mere meta-jiffy instead.

*The Metaverse Dictionary*

**Meta-wet,** *adj.* As dry as software.

**Meta-whipping,** *v.t.* A whipping that doesn't hurt a bit, but it still might be mentally devastating. Perhaps, a tongue-lashing with visual special effects.

**Meta-whisper,** *v.t.* Meta-words that are said as if quietly, like you are intimating a secret, but that all the surveillance at every level still records, . . . for your convenience.

**Meta-whistle,** *v.i., n.* Pushing the "Whistle" button.

**Meta-white,** *adj.* Still, the default color for the background of text.

**Meta-wife,** *n.* That woman you married, but hardly ever see in-person (perhaps because of your meta-jobs). [See Meta-husband.]

**Meta-win,** *v.* Success, as measure by the criteria set for your simulation, online game, or meta-world.

**Meta-wipe,** *v.t.* Smear, blur, or clear away many meta-things with a single action.

**Meta-wire,** *n.* "Greetings. Stop." Or, a text message.

**Meta-wit,** *n.* A talent for banter about the Metaverse. Or, a talent for thinking.

**Meta-woes,** *n.* Misadventures, but hopefully of the kind that can just be abandoned or deleted.

**Meta-Wonder,** *n.* Perhaps, a super-meta-hero type in a meta-world. Or, someone that can leap from meta-world to meta-world in a single bound.

**Meta-wonderful,** *adj.* Probably wonderful. You may never know about the deep dark meta-secrets.

*The Metaverse Dictionary*

**Meta-wondering,** *v.i.* Hoping the speaker will elaborate more on the subject of your meta-interest.

**Meta-wood,** *n.* Really, meta-plastic.

**Meta-word,** *n.* A hyphenated word (for example, a compound-noun, such as this one) that has the word "meta" as a prefix. Or, a word or phrase that is not quite understood because it has not been explained clearly enough. [See Meta-speak.]

**Meta-work,** *n.* The kind of work that is only available in a meta-environment like a simulation, online game, shopping site, and meta-world. Or, the kind of work that is involved in bringing parts of the Metaverse into existence. Or, the kind of work that most would call "thinking." [See Meta-job, Meta-method.]

**Meta-world,** *n.* An online environment that has structures and boundaries that make it distinct from other places in the Metaverse.

**Meta-write,** *v.t.* To write in a meta-space. Or, to write about the Metaverse.

**Meta-wrong,** *adj.* Perhaps, wrong for almost-here.

# X

**Meta-xenophobe,** *n.* One unduly fearful of what is real, and especially of real people in the real world and what they can do.

**Meta-Xmas,** *n.* Any celebration in the Metaverse preceded by a month of product advertisements, and the singing of "Frosty the Snowman." Gifts may be of any size, or shape, or complexity. New life forms may emerge during this season. Meta-characters from the past may also show up. Meta-Xmas is actually a two-day event, because of the way time-zones work. Same as New Years.

**Meta-xylophone,** *n.* A fake instrument that when played may sound like anything, . . . or nothing at all.

*The Metaverse Dictionary*

# Y

**Meta-yacht,** *n.* A personal meta-watercraft that seems to be fairly large. You go aboard, and it has a bath, furniture, a wet bar, working ship-to-shore communications, an anchor, and sufficient crew, . . . and it still may or may not resemble the kind of yacht that you might find in the real world.

**Meta-yard,** *n.* A place for your fake dog to take a clean poop – in any color that you select from a menu.

**Meta-yawn,** *n., v.i.* A stifled yawn, like the ones that occur in important business meeting.

**Meta-yawp,** *n., v.i.* A cry, yelp, or squawk uttered by such a small animal that you barely hear it.

**Meta-year,** *n.* The length of time it take for twelve meta-months to go by in a simulation.

**Meta-yellow,** *adj.* The color yellow, just done with software. (A good color for meta-kitchen meta-walls.)

**Meta-yes,** *adv., n.* Probably. Tomorrow. Or, "Let me see if I can think of a reason why not."

**Meta-yesterday,** *adv., n.* Whatever's in the can.

**Meta-yield,** *n.* The results of a meta-process – which may or may not be noticeable to you depending on settings, filters, and privileges.

**Meta-yoke,** *n.* When the yoke is on a meta-ewe.

*The Metaverse Dictionary*

**Meta-yoo-hoo,** *interj.* "Hey," or "Y'all." Perhaps, heard louder and farther than one might expect.

**Meta-yoot,** *n.* Perhaps, a tween, or a teenager, or a very old bot.

**Meta-young,** *adj.* Anyone, . . . if or when they choose to appear or sound young.

**Meta-yuppie,** *adj., n.* Virtually everybody. Who would not want to be a young urban professional in the Metaverse. This is one meta-thing that may meta-unite most of us.

# Z

**Meta-zany,** *adj.* If you think zany is ludicrous, exaggerated, or unprincipled in the real world, wait until you see the meta-versions. Nobody likes the meta-mainstream. Most meta-sit coms have meta-zany characters. Meta-actors are encouraged to be meta-zany in their real personal lives too, but not so zany that they become meta-unemployable. If you yourself ever go meta-zany, you might find it difficult to get out of your own meta-way.

**Meta-zeal,** *n.* Zeal for Metaverse stuff.

**Meta-zirconia,** *n.* A less-expensive alternative to cubic-zirconia.

**Meta-zone,** *n.* Where your mind goes while you are using meta-words and meta-speak. Or, the inside of any store that sells meta-stuff. Or, a zone in the Metaverse. [See Meta-think, Meta-mug, Meta-shirt.]

**Meta-zoo,** *n.* A fake place with fake animals where real people spend real time. Still, don't try to stick your meta-head inside the meta-lion's meta-mouth (just in case).

**Meta-zoom,** *v.i., n.* An almost-magical magnifying facility such that bits and bytes are made to look like like Mandelbrot sets, paramecium, elephants, and galaxies.

**Meta-zygote,** *n.* A few meta-cells that together can turn into anything, . . . meta-naturally.

*The Metaverse Dictionary*

None of what is not on this page was deleted by mistake.

*The Metaverse Dictionary*

Of course, there could be more here. And there probably will be in the next edition.

www.ingramcontent.com/pod-product-compliance
Lightning Source LLC
Chambersburg PA
CBHW061451040426
42450CB00007B/1316